Cambridge Elements

Elements in Data Rights and Wrongs
edited by
Damian Clifford
Australian National University
Jeannie Marie Paterson
University of Melbourne

ADDRESSING MISINFORMATION AND DISINFORMATION

James Meese
RMIT University
Corinne Tan
National University of Singapore

CAMBRIDGE
UNIVERSITY PRESS

CAMBRIDGE
UNIVERSITY PRESS

Shaftesbury Road, Cambridge CB2 8EA, United Kingdom

One Liberty Plaza, 20th Floor, New York, NY 10006, USA

477 Williamstown Road, Port Melbourne, VIC 3207, Australia

314–321, 3rd Floor, Plot 3, Splendor Forum, Jasola District Centre,
New Delhi – 110025, India

Cambridge University Press is part of Cambridge University Press & Assessment,
a department of the University of Cambridge.

We share the University's mission to contribute to society through the pursuit of
education, learning and research at the highest international levels of excellence.

www.cambridge.org
Information on this title: www.cambridge.org/9781009768153

DOI: 10.1017/9781009768177

When citing this work, please include a reference to the DOI 10.1017/9781009768177

First published 2026

A catalogue record for this publication is available from the British Library

A Cataloging-in-Publication data record for this Element is available from the Library of Congress

ISBN 978-1-009-76816-0 Hardback
ISBN 978-1-009-76815-3 Paperback
ISSN 2976-7520 (online)
ISSN 2976-7512 (print)

Addressing Misinformation and Disinformation

Elements in Data Rights and Wrongs

DOI: 10.1017/9781009768177
First published online: February 2026

James Meese
RMIT University

Corinne Tan
National University of Singapore

Author for correspondence: James Meese, james.meese@rmit.edu.au

Abstract: Concerns around misinformation and disinformation have intensified with the rise of AI tools, with many claiming this is a watershed moment for truth, accuracy and democracy. In response, numerous laws have been enacted in different jurisdictions. *Addressing Misinformation and Disinformation* introduces this new legal landscape and charts a path forward. The Element identifies avoidance or alleviation of harm as a central legal preoccupation, outlines technical developments associated with AI and other technologies, and highlights social approaches that can support long-term civic resilience. Offering an expansive interdisciplinary analysis that moves beyond narrow debates about definitions, *Addressing Misinformation and Disinformation* shows how law can work alongside other technical and social mechanisms, as part of a coherent policy response.

Keywords: misinformation, disinformation, AI, Regulation, Platforms

ISBNs: 9781009768160 (HB), 9781009768153 (PB), 9781009768177 (OC)
ISSNs: 2976-7520 (online), 2976-7512 (print)

Contents

Introduction

The circulation of doubtful, contestable or outright false information with harmful effects, and indeed sometimes intent, is a serious problem that the world has long endured.[1] But it has emerged as a significant societal challenge in recent years. Since the mid-2010s, a range of actors – from policymakers and politicians to civil society groups and myriad individuals – have raised concerns about the amount of misinformation and disinformation spreading across the internet, especially (but not only) in the hands of malicious actors. Information circulating during the COVID-19 pandemic amplified public anxieties and highlighted the risks associated with its societal impacts. More recently, fears about misinformation and disinformation (commonly described as misinformation with malicious intent) have increased following the widespread availability of inexpensive and easy-to-use artificial intelligence (AI) tools.[2]

Older laws, including laws around defamation, privacy and data protection, fraud, deceptive acts or practices, free and fair elections, copyright and other intellectual property, are already being used to address some of these concerns. However, many states have not been comfortable relying on these and have passed additional laws. According to one study, more than half the countries of the world now have laws addressing misinformation or disinformation (Chesterman, 2025). Some are very tailored. For instance, some states have introduced, or are in the process of introducing, laws around hate speech, sexually explicitly deepfakes, political interference and scams. The United States is an example with its TAKE IT DOWN Act of 2025 geared to sexually explicit deepfakes. Others are broader in focus, as with the European Union's Digital Services Act (DSA) of 2022 and Artificial Intelligence Act of 2024 (AI Act) and the United Kingdom's Online Safety Act (OSA) of 2023. Australia and Singapore, our home countries, offer further interesting examples.

Nevertheless, the argument of this Element is that the new laws, and indeed law more generally, will not be sufficient to address the diverse harms

[1] Given this long history, and the vague nature of many current definitions, we adopt a deliberately broad ambit in defining these types of information as 'misinformation or disinformation'. We place focus explicitly on harms associated with their circulation. For a recent situated account of the definitional challenges, see Evelyn Douek (2025) on medical misinformation.

[2] There is an extensive literature on the impact of AI in this area (as in others) (see, for instance, Bontridder and Poullet, 2021; Birrer and Just, 2024; Marchal et al., 2024; Chesterman, 2025). While much attention has focussed on AI's role in generating information, we note that it can also have a significant role in distributing information (see, for instance, Meese and Bannerman, 2022).

associated with misinformation and disinformation. Of course, it is too soon to assess the impact of all the current and still-to-be created laws. But one problem that is already evident is that while information easily spreads across the internet, the laws that seek to address its harms tend to be national or (in the case of the EU) regional in character. Another is that, for all the talk of 'rights' in this area, the harms of misinformation and disinformation may be differently perceived in different parts of the world, as may be the harms associated with efforts to regulate it. For instance, what in Europe may be considered a proportionate legal response to the harms of hate speech under the DSA, building on the EU Charter of Fundamental Rights (2000), may in the US be viewed as impacting overly negatively on innovation and on free speech protected by the First Amendment (US Judiciary Committee Staff Report, 2025). A third, less noticed, problem is that even where laws may be good at deterring harmful conduct, they may do little to address the underlying social causes and build social resilience for the future. In short, we argue that while many jurisdictions have turned to legal solutions to address harms, which we go on to detail, these reform agendas can often dominate the policy conversation, leaving little air for the technical developments and social approaches that support long-term civic resilience.

The remainder of this Element represents our attempt as respectively media studies and legal scholars to advance the earlier arguments in greater detail. In Section 1, we track some of the current and emerging laws with a goal of understanding some of the actual and anticipated harms they seek to avoid or alleviate, and the ways they go about this. In Section 2, we then move on to technical efforts by digital platforms to address harmful misinformation and disinformation. Here, we explore how digital platforms are using technical systems and the extent to which these can be used to address harmful misinformation and disinformation. Some of these measures may be changing as we write, but they exemplify various currents at work. Finally, we end with our argument for exploring the role that social approaches and tools can play.

1 Proliferating Laws

1.1 Perceived Need for Legal Intervention

This section considers the growing array of legislative efforts geared (in whole or in part) to addressing the harms of misinformation and disinformation. In terms of the sheer number of enactments, these laws are noteworthy. For instance, a study conducted by Gabrielle Lim and Samantha Bradshaw for the Center for International Media Assistance and the National Endowment for Democracy reports that, globally, ninety-one items of legislation were enacted between 2016 and 2022 to address misinformation and disinformation (Lim and Bradshaw, 2023). Another study from Simon Chesterman at the National University of Singapore reports that, as at the start of 2024, more than half the countries of the world had adopted laws designed to 'reduce the impact of false or malicious information online' (Chesterman, 2025: 934).

While touched on in the second study, we pay particular attention in this section to two significant pieces of regional and national legislation adopted in 2022 and 2023 which are geared specifically to platforms that host and circulate misinformation and disinformation posted by users, namely the EU DSA and the UK OSA. (The Australian version of the OSA was passed in 2021, albeit in more restricted form.) As Chesterman points out, and as we come back to later, in practice 'much [in this space] has depended on technical interventions by platforms' (Chesterman, 2025: 944). Laws such as the DSA and OSA provide some legal oversight but bring their jurisdictions into sharp relief with the US where § 230 of the Communications Decency Act (CDA) of 1999 provides that platforms are generally immunised from legally responsibility for content posted by users,[3] and 'good Samaritan' interventions by platforms are further protected from legal responsibility (Chesterman, 2025: 946).

Another focus of this section is the EU AI Act of 2024, with its provisions currently scheduled to come into operation in stages from February 2025 to August 2027. This will also impact on (some) AI-fuelled misinformation and disinformation. Indeed, its impact could be very significant, although its precise reach is still not clear with much depending on how the provisions (once in force) are deployed in practice (see Duivenvoorde, 2025). But the EU is not the only jurisdiction to address AI-related misinformation and disinformation specifically, even if its AI Act is the most comprehensive legislation to date. For instance, in the US now, there is new federal legislation in the form of the TAKE IT DOWN Act of 2025 to address sexually explicit deepfakes (see Ortutay, 2025). Other laws, such as Singapore's Protection from Online Falsehoods and Manipulation Act of 2019 (POFMA), are broad enough in their terms to address deepfakes (Shanmugam, 2024).

[3] This is subject to limited exceptions: for federal criminal law, intellectual property, electronic privacy and sex trafficking. Note that the language of § 230(c)(1) ('No provider or user of an interactive computer service shall be treated as the publisher or speaker of any information provided by another information content provider') does not exonerate platforms from responsibility for content they provide.

No doubt there will be more legislative efforts to come in this space. Some may be controversial, as indeed are many of the legislative efforts noted previously. However, in this section we do not seek to critique particular legislative initiatives (see, for instance, Coe, 2023 on the OSA), or particular types or features of legislation (for a comprehensive review, see Katsirea, 2024), or the definitional challenges of embedding vague terms such as 'misinformation' and 'disinformation' into law (see Roberts et al., 2025; OECD, 2024: 17), or the fact of using legislation to manage what some might say is 'a sense of urgency expressed in polemical terms' (Burgess, 2023). Instead, we think it is useful to treat misinformation and disinformation as a problem that can lead to real harms and then consider broadly the legislation being introduced to address concerns around these harms. At the same time, we acknowledge concerns about actual and potential impacts of these laws on other rights, freedoms and interests, such as freedom of speech and innovation. And we point out the limits of these laws, even if well designed to address misinformation and disinformation in a properly balanced, or 'proportionate', way – and of law in general.

1.2 Continuing Reliance on Older Laws

Of course, the new laws do not operate in a vacuum. Older laws continue to regulate and their significance should not be underestimated. For instance, users of Facebook successfully settled class action claims in California *inter alia* for breach of various privacy torts and negligence following Cambridge Analytica's harvesting of their data to target political and commercial advertising without their knowledge or consent (In Re Facebook, Inc. Consumer Privacy User Profile Litigation, 2018). Such torts might also be drawn on to address AI-related practices. Indeed, some have suggested that AI was already being used by Cambridge Analytica in 2016 (see Delcker, 2020). More recently Scarlett Johansson's legal dispute with OpenAI after its launch of an AI-generated voice in ChatGPT 'eerily' resembling her own is reminiscent of the earlier California right of publicity case *Midler* v *Ford Motor Co* where Bette Midler succeeded in arguing that the use of a soundalike voice in Ford advertising for a nostalgic line of cars was a violation of her common law right of publicity under California law (*Midler* v *Ford Motor Co*, 1998).[4] Open AI has since reluctantly withdrawn the soundalike voice (Robins-Early, 2024). Further, in *Starbucks* v

[4] For the potential use of US copyright and trademarks law to address deepfakes (and the impact of the proposed NO FAKES Act of 2025), see Ginsburg and Austin (2025).

Meta Platforms (2025), conservative activist Robby Starbuck successfully claimed defamation against Meta for disseminating false statements about his participation in the capital riot of January 2021, among other false statements, via its chatbot Meta AI, resulting in a settlement (see *Starbuck* v Meta Platforms, Inc., 2025; Volokh, 2025a). Starbuck has followed up with another complaint of defamation against Google, alleging that the company spread 'outrageously false' lies through its AI products (Volokh, 2025b).

Misinformation and disinformation in trade or commerce may also be targeted under consumer protection laws such as the Federal Trade Commission Act (FTCA) in the US (specifically, its § 5 prohibition on 'unfair or deceptive acts or practices'), the Australian Consumer Law (ACL) of 2010 in Australia (including its s 18 prohibition on misleading or deceptive conduct), and the EU Unfair Commercial Practices Directive (UCPD) of 2005 in Europe (see Federal Trade Commission, 2024; Harding, Paterson and Bant, 2022; Duivendoorde, 2025). Fraud may also be claimed in egregious cases.[5] Already, there are examples. For instance, following the Cambridge Analytica scandal, in 2019 Facebook was fined a record $5b by the Federal Trade Commission (FTC) for deceiving users about their ability to keep personal information private (FTC, 2019a), and Cambridge Analytica was prohibited from making further misrepresentations (FTC 2019b). A securities fraud claim launched by investors against Mark Zuckerberg and others has also been settled (Associated Press, 2025). The FTC further has responsibility for the US Children's Online Privacy Protection Act (COPPA) 1998, requiring parental consent for children (under 13 years) to access commercial websites and online services. As such, COPPA in a sense protects children from online misinformation and disinformation, although its remit is much broader. The same may be said of the Australian social media ban for children (under 16 years) in the Online Safety Amendment (Social Media Minimum Age) Act 2024, in force from December 2025.

Data protection laws establishing standards for the processing of personal data may also be relied on to address the generation and spread of misinformation and disinformation within their compasses.[6] The EU General Data Protection Regulation (GDPR) 2016 could well prove to be

[5] Including as a matter of criminal laws (see Chesterman, 2025: 938, although noting the practical difficulties of bringing claims, including against fraudsters operating from outside the jurisdiction).

[6] We include in this category US style 'data privacy' laws, for instance the federal Video Privacy Protection Act (VPPA) which was the basis of another claim in the *In Re Facebook Consumer Privacy Profile Litigation* class action noted earlier; the Illinois Biometric Information Privacy Act 2008 (BIPA) addressing the collection and use of (sensitive) biometric data; and the California Consumer Privacy Act (2018) and California Privacy

especially powerful, given its design as a comprehensive modern regime (see Yeung and Bygrave, 2021). Its impact can be seen already in certain cases, including a recent case against Google where the European Court of Justice (CJEU) held that the right of erasure/right to be forgotten in article 17 GDPR may be drawn on to require dereferencing by search engines of 'manifestly inaccurate' personal data in breach of article 5(1)(d), under specified conditions (*TU and RE* v *Google LLC*, 2022).[7] But other regimes may also provide important protections, either directly through their accuracy requirements for data processing or indirectly through other standards applied to data processing of personal data. To give just one example, in Illinois, a class action lawsuit launched under the Biometric Information Privacy Act 2008 (BIPA) in relation to Clearview AI's generation and dissemination of profiles harvested from biometric face images on the internet, for use by Clearview's commercial customers including in law enforcement, was recently settled (*In Re Clearview AI* Consumer Privacy Litigation, 2025). Although the non-consensual processing of individuals' biometric data was the main legal foundation of the BIPA claims, the court noted as 'not wholly without merit' the concern expressed by the American Civil Liberties Union (ACLU) that 'numerous studies have shown that face recognition technology misidentifies Black people and other people of colour at higher rates than white people' leading to 'higher incidence of wrongful arrest' (*In Re Clearview AI* Consumer Privacy Litigation, 2025: 32).[8]

Also worth noting are electoral laws which may be drawn on to deal with current issues of misinformation and disinformation in election contexts. For instance, in Australia, in the lead-up to the May 2025 federal election, the Australian Electoral Commission established under the Commonwealth Electoral Act 1918 (Cth) launched a 'Stop and Consider' campaign urging Australian voters to pause and reflect on 'information being distributed which is seeking to influence your vote', to ask questions such as whether it is from 'a reliable or recognisable source', and whether it

Rights Act (2020) (which, although still quite ambiguous and contested, according to Pasquale 2025a: 28–33, offer an important source of protection in that state).

7 For a further case pending against ChatGPT, concerning its apparent 'hallucination' that Norwegian Arve Hjalmar Holmen had been convicted of murdering two of his children and attempting to kill a third, see the complaint filed with the Danish Data Protection Agency by the data protection/data privacy advocacy group None of Your Business (NYOB) (NYOB, 2025a; NPYB, 2025b).

8 See also, in a determination made by the Australian Commissioner under the Australian Privacy Act 1988 (Cth), also referring to the risks associated with inaccurate Clearview AI biometric profiles, *Commissioner Initiated Investigation into Clearview AI, Inc (Privacy)*, 2021: [217]).

could 'be a scam', and stressed the AEC's role in providing reliable information on the electoral process and in investigating complaints (AEC, 2025; see Grantham, 2025). In other countries, more concrete steps have been taken under existing political advertising laws. For instance, in the US the Federal Communications Commission (FCC) which has responsibility for telephone and broadcast communication, determined that the US Telephone Consumer Protection Act (TCPA) of 1991 extends to telephone calls that use or include AI-generated voices, and in September 2024 fined a political consultant $6 million over robocalls that mimicked President Joe Biden's voice, urging New Hampshire voters not to vote in that state's Democratic primary (FCC, 2024a).

The developments discussed earlier suggest that older laws (including some laws that are not all that old and are still being interpreted and updated) will continue to be looked to in this context, as in others. At the very least, they highlight the flexibility of established legal frameworks and doctrines that may be called on to address misinformation and disinformation. In some, perhaps even many, instances they provide a way to address these, while still providing a balance with free speech and innovation.

We now turn to newer laws, which have been designed (at least in part) to deal with misinformation and disinformation, and their associated harms.

1.3 Newer Laws

As a preliminary comment, we note that, while most jurisdictions view misinformation and disinformation and their harms as problems that requires a definite legal solution, there is little consistency in terms of the scope and range of the new laws that are emerging (including whether they should be framed in broader or narrower terms, and whether their focus should be primarily on misinformation and/or disinformation, or rather on harm, or on some combination of these) and their balances with freedom of speech and innovation. Table 1 presents examples of legislative initiatives in selected jurisdictions over the last five to six years. We then move on to consider some of the types of harms that these laws seek to address (in either specific terms or as part of a broader sweep), focussing on hate speech, sexually explicit deepfakes, political interference, and scams,[9] although we still note considerable variations between jurisdictions as to whether, when, and how these should be regulated.

[9] These are not the only possible examples. For instance, laws targeting public health misinformation, which saw a spike during the Covid pandemic are another (Chesterman, 2025: 936).

Table 1 Examples of New Laws

Jurisdiction	Laws	Scope	Measures
Singapore	Protection from Online Falsehoods and Manipulation Act 2019 (POFMA)	Online circulation of false information contrary to the public interest, with specific provision made for 'co-ordinated inauthentic behaviour'	Directions ranging from corrections to stop communication, or for internet access service providers to block access (POFMA Office)
	Online Safety (Miscellaneous Amendments) Act 2022	Online circulation of 'egregious' and other harmful content' (as specified) – with priority placed on the protection of children	Directions to stop communication, or for online platforms to disable access (Info-communications Media Development Authority (IMDA))
	Online Criminal Harms Act 2023 (OCHA) and Protection from Scams Act 2025 (PSA)	Scams	The OCHA requires online platforms to adopt measures to proactively disrupt online scams; the PSA allows for restriction orders from the police to block credit facilities
Australia	Online Safety Act 2021 (Australian OSA)	Online circulation of intimate images, cyber-abuse content (under narrowly specified conditions), and cyber-bullying content harmful to children	Provides for takedown mechanism and other measures (e-Safety Commissioner)
	Criminal Code Amendment (Deepfake Sexual Material) Act 2024	Creation and circulation of sexually explicit deepfakes	Criminal penalties
	Scams Prevention Framework Act 2025	Online scams	Provides a framework for preventing and responding to scams

EU	Digital Services Act 2022 (DSA)	Online circulation of unlawful or otherwise harmful content (as indicated in general terms)	Requires takedown mechanism for online platforms (for illegal content), as well as risk assessments and mitigation for very large online platforms (VLOPs) and very large online search engines (VLOSEs)
	Artificial Intelligence Act 2024 (AI Act)	Provision and deployment of certain AI systems (as specified), including deepfakes	Requires minimal transparency protections such as labelling
		Provision and deployment of 'high-risk AI systems', as well as AI practices that pose 'unacceptable risks', for example placing on the market, putting into service or use of an AI system that 'deploys purposefully manipulative or deceptive techniques', or 'exploits the vulnerabilities' of natural persons or groups, including children, in a manner that causes or is reasonably likely to cause 'significant harm' (under specified conditions)	Additional layers of regulation, and even bans in the most serious cases of 'unacceptable risks'
	Regulation on the Transparency and Targeting of Political Advertising 2024 (TTPA)	Political advertising	Requires labelling; and imposes standards for targeting of political advertising online

(Continued)

Table 1 (Continued)

Jurisdiction	Laws	Scope	Measures
UK	Online Safety Act 2023 (UK OSA)	Creation and online circulation of illegal harmful content, or in the case of children harmful content	Requires online platforms to proactively remove content and to minimise risk. Guided by Office of Communications (Ofcom)
	New offences to come with the Crime and Policing Bill 2025	Creation and circulation of sexually explicit deepfakes	Criminal penalties
US	Tools to Address Known Exploitation by Immobilizing Technological Deepfakes on Websites and Networks (TAKE IT DOWN) Act 2025	Circulation of non-consensual intimate imagery, including sexually explicit deepfakes	Criminalises and requires timely takedown from 'covered platforms' on valid request

1.3.1 Hate Speech

Hate speech was an early focus of new efforts at legal regulation, including in Europe, with some adopting strongly interventionist approaches. An example is the now superseded German Network Enforcement Act (or NetzDG, 2017), which required platforms with over two million users to allow users to report content easily, remove 'manifestly unlawful' content within twenty-four hours, remove unlawful content within seven days, and produce transparency reports. Following NetzDG, amendments to the Russian Federal Statute 'On Information, Information Technologies and Protection of Information' (or the IT Law) and the Code on Administrative Offences were made in 2017, empowering the federal executive body (or Roskomnadzor, part of the Ministry of Digital Development, Communication and Mass Media) to monitor relevant online content, determine whether certain content essential to the public was false, and to obligate news aggregators to stop disseminating such information (Rumyantsev, 2017). Other comparable laws have been identified in Pakistan, Turkey and other countries with various political challenges such as authoritarian governments, persistent challenges with free speech, a lack of competitive elections, or a combination of all three (Meese and Hurcombe, 2020; Canaan, 2022).

NetzDG is now superseded by the EU DSA 2022 which adopts an overarching risk-based approach to platform liability for third-party content posted on the platform, paying particular attention to rights protected in the EU Charter of Fundamental Rights (2000). Specifically, articles 34 and 35 DSA require 'very large online platforms' (VLOPs), such as YouTube, LinkedIn, Facebook, Instagram, TikTok and X, and 'very large online search engines' (VLOSEs), such as Google (article 33 DSA; European Commission, 2025a) to engage in risk assessment and mitigation (Husovec, 2024a, 2024b).[10] Article 34 requires VLOPs and VLOSEs to conduct ongoing assessments and analysis of their systems, including algorithmic systems, or from the use made of their systems, to identify systemic risks around the dissemination of illegal content through their services, actual or foreseeable negative effects on civic discourse and public security, and negative consequences to a person's physical and mental well-being. Article 35 obligates VLOPs and VLOSEs to implement a range of tailored measures to mitigate a variety of systemic

[10] Note that, while generally in this Element we use 'platforms' as a broadly encompassing term covering also search engines, the DSA distinguishes between platforms and search engines.

risks, from adjusting their algorithmic systems (article 35(1)(d)) to adapting their terms and conditions (article 35(1)(b)). Martin Husovec argues that the European Commission did not set out to become a 'Ministry of Truth' (Husovec, 2024a: 48), and that the law's aim was to function as a broader effort to support a positive online ecosystem rather than authorising government actors to restrict specific forms of legal speech, based on their conceptions of harm (Husovec, 2024a: 56). However, on its face, the DSA can regulate content deemed harmful, including hate speech through the risk management and transparency measures it imposes on VLOPs and VLOSEs (and through its required takedown mechanism which is directed at illegal content). On the whole, the DSA offers an interesting co-regulatory model in its efforts to conscript VLOPs and VLOSEs to act as ultimate authorities in the regulation of misinformation and disinformation on these platforms (see generally Husovec, 2024a, 2024b; Kenyon, 2024).

On top of that, the EU AI Act of 2024 adopts a risk-based approach to the regulation of hate speech (along with other types of harmful speech), including hate speech involving misinformation and disinformation generated through AI systems. In brief, while AI systems considered to be low risk are subject to minimal transparency regulation under article 50 of the AI Act, 'high-risk' AI systems that are deemed to pose serious risks to health, safety or fundamental rights are subject to higher regulation under articles 6–15. Practices that are deemed an 'unacceptable risk' are banned if they fall within the categories listed in article 5 (and meet the conditions specified). Examples include the placing on the market, or putting into service or the use of an AI system that 'deploys … purposefully manipulative or deceptive techniques' impacting on conduct or decision-making of individuals or groups a manner that causes or is reasonably likely to cause 'significant harm' (article 5(1)(a)), or 'exploits any of the vulnerabilities of a natural person or a specific group of persons', such as children, in a manner that causes or is reasonably likely to cause 'significant harm' (article 5(1(b))).

Compare the UK OSA: although its focus, except where children are affected, is illegal harmful speech, there are other UK hate speech laws.[11] Singapore's POFMA is framed more broadly in terms of addressing online falsehoods and manipulation in the public interest (see Tan, 2022a;

[11] The UK's Public Order Act 1986 and Racial and Religious Hatred Act 2006 prohibit the use of abusive and insulting language inciting hatred and violence against individuals based on protected characteristics such as race, religion or sexual orientation.

Chen, 2023), with further protections for children *via* the Online Safety (Miscellaneous Amendments) Act 2022. The Australian OSA's protections against circulation of cyber-abuse material directed at adults and cyber-bullying material directed at children likewise catches some hate speech involving misinformation and disinformation.[12] Moreover, the Australian OSA's provisions for takedown of non-consensual intimate images (s 35) may be viewed as addressing one particular type of 'gendered hate speech' (see Suzor, Seignior and Singleton, 2017: 1092), and the Criminal Code Amendment (Deepfake Sexual Material) Act 2024 provides further criminal penalties. Likewise, the UK's Crime and Policing Bill 2025 will introduce new offences covering sexually explicit deepfakes and will further expand the remit of the UK OSA to address what may be viewed as gendered hate speech. The same may be said of the criminalisation of the non-consensual publication of intimate images including sexually explicit deepfakes under the US TAKE IT DOWN Act. Although hate speech has generally not been subject to regulation in the US where the constitutional free speech mandate of the First Amendment is considered to be very broad (Kenyon, 2024; Chesterman, 2025: 947 n 83) and the legal scope for assigning platform responsibility is limited by § 230 CDA, the TAKE IT DOWN Act is an apparent derogation framed for the current environment (see Wihbey, 2025a).

Such laws reflect the overlap when addressing what may be called 'gendered hate speech' with the next category of sexually explicit (and other) deepfakes.

1.3.2 Sexually Explicit Deepfakes

The deepfake non-consensual sexual imagery example is particularly concerning in social terms because, according to some estimates, 90–95% of deepfake videos involve non-consensual pornographic videos and, of those videos, 90% target women (Hao 2021). Even the US, a country reluctant to regulate misinformation or disinformation based on content due to perceived First Amendment restraints (as well as concerns about the likely impact on innovation), has introduced reforms directly targeting the problem of sexually explicit deepfakes and other intimate visual content posted online without consent in the form of the TAKE IT DOWN Act passed in the Senate in December 2024, in the House in January 2025, and signed by President Donald Trump in March 2025 (Croft, 2024;

[12] More may be caught if the proposed Online Safety Amendment (Digital Duty of Care) Bill 2024 (Cth) (extending the duties of platforms) is enacted.

Ortutay, 2025). The Act criminalises the non-consensual publication of intimate images of an identifiable individual, including specific provisions for 'authentic visual depictions' of children and requires measures from 'covered platforms' to take down deepfakes and other non-consensual intimate images upon receipt of valid complaints (with the latter coming into effect in May 2026).[13] Some states have gone further in regulating the production and distribution of deepfake non-consensual sexual imagery. For example, California amended its penal code to criminalise the distribution of 'photo realistic image, digital image, electronic image [...] of an intimate body part [...] engaged in specified sexual acts, that was created in a manner that would cause a reasonable person to believe the image is an authentic image' (CA Penal Code, 2024: § 647(j)(4)(A)(ii)). Numerous other states have followed suit including Washington, Florida and Utah (NCSL, 2024).

Similar trends towards addressing deepfakes can be seen in other jurisdictions, although with considerable variation as to the scope of the laws and the measures deployed. The EU DSA addresses non-consensual circulation on digital platforms of sexually explicit deepfakes through its takedown mechanism (article 16) and may also address a wider range of deemed-to-be harmful deepfakes through its content moderation processes (article 35). The AI Act requires AI deepfakes to be labelled under article 50 and generally adopts an approach that low-risk AI systems are to be minimally regulated through transparency requirements (see Fragale and Grilli, 2024), although higher-risk AI systems may be more highly regulated (articles 6 to 15), and practices deemed 'unacceptable risk' (under article 5, already in operation) – and this may, of course, apply to some practices involving the use of deepfakes.[14] In Australia, as noted earlier, the creation and sharing of 'non-consensual deepfake sexually explicit material' by individuals has been criminalised under the Criminal Code Amendment (Deepfake Sexual Material) Act 2024 (s 5, substituting s 474.17A of the Criminal Code). Further, the non-consensual sharing of

[13] Further reform is proposed. The US Senate, in July 2025, passed the Disrupt Explicit Forged Images and Non-Consensual Edits (DEFIANCE) Act, which would give victims of non-consensual deepfake pornography the power to commence civil actions against the perpetrators who make or distribute such imagery (Shapero and Nazzaro, 2025). In January 2025 the Bill lapsed, having failed to pass the House of Representatives. But in May 2025, the Bill was reintroduced (Durbin, 2025).

[14] Labelling is also a regulatory approach adopted in China with its 2025 Notice on issuing 'Measures for the Identification of Artificial Intelligence-Generated Synthetic Content', *inter alia* seeking to combat harmful deepfakes by requiring labelling (Cyberspace Administration of China, 2023).

intimate images (including deepfakes) is regulated under the Australian OSA (s 75) and jurisdiction is given to the e-Safety Commissioner to require the images to be removed (s 27 and ss 77–78) and to take proceedings to court for penalties. This power has already been used in one case in Australia, concerning the posting by a Queensland man of deepfake images of high-profile Australian women, and a penalty of $343,500 (Australian dollars) was ordered (*eSafety Commissioner* v Rotondo, 2025). The UK's Online Safety Act of 2023 (UK OSA) also provides for penalties, as well as setting out a procedure for requiring online platforms to remove content that is illegal and harmful (or, in the case of children, harmful) under Ofcom's oversight (ss 2, 10, 12–13, and pt. 7), including with respect to non-consensual sharing of intimate images including deepfakes.[15] Criminal provisions and penalties to supplement the UK OSA's regulation are being introduced under the Crime and Policing bill 2025 which will criminalise the making and sharing of intimate deepfakes.

1.3.3 Political Interference

Chesterman notes that an early and still common focus of laws around misinformation and disinformation is 'on national security broadly construed' (Chesterman, 2025: 936). There is little general federal regulation of misinformation and disinformation in political advertising in the US, especially in the online environment, with the First Amendment often cited as a reason (see Caplan, 2024; Pasquale, 2025b) and the CDA § 230 another consideration. Regardless, various states in the US have introduced reforms addressing the use of deepfakes and other AI-related misinformation and disinformation in election campaigning (see citizen.org tracker (2025) for a list). Many of these reforms have centred around disclosure and transparency requirements.[16] For example, in Michigan, New Hampshire and New York (among others), the use of AI in political advertising needs to simply be disclosed. California offered a more systemic response under the Defending Democracy from Deepfake Deception Act of 2024, requiring an online platform to 'block the posting or sending of materially deceptive and digitally modified or created content related to elections, during certain periods before and after an election' (NCSL, 2024). However, the latter was struck down in August 2025 for violation

[15] Specifically, the UK OSA s 188 created a new offence of sharing intimate images (including deepfakes) via a new s 66B Sexual Offences Act 2003.

[16] The FCC has proposed disclosure rules for the use of AI in political advertising, but these would extend only to radio and television political advertisements (FCC, 2024b).

of the CDA § 230, without pronouncing on the First Amendment issue (see Spoto, 2025).

Singapore, under amendments to elections laws in 2024, now criminalises 'the publication of online content that realistically depicts a candidate saying or doing something that … [the candidate] did not' over critical election periods (see Chin, 2024). Singapore's POFMA has additionally been deployed against (what is deemed to be) misinformation or disinformation in political advertising, drawing on the powers of the POFMA office to issue directions for correction of false statements made or, in more extreme cases, to stop communication of statements or block access to online locations (POFMA, 2019: parts 3 to 6). Because the High Court is precluded from exercising judicial review regarding whether a falsehood undermines public interest, safeguards against the wrongful issuance of directions under POFMA are suggested to be weak (Tan and Teng, 2020). And, more generally, the limited scope to raise free speech concerns has made the regime controversial, with some arguing that at very least its potential for censorship merits further study (Teo, 2021).[17]

The EU DSA has also been used to address political interference involving misinformation and disinformation, and the results have also proved to be controversial. For instance, in early 2024, the European Commission required digital platforms to show how they plan to address deepfakes, following evidence of Russian interference in elections (O'Carroll and Hern, 2024). Later, in December 2024, the Commission followed up with formal proceedings against TikTok to investigate whether the platform appropriately managed electoral risks in Romania after the failed election there, alongside allegations of interference (using TikTok) by Russia (Albert, 2024; Radu, 2025). The political consequences of the revelations were felt in the May 2025 election, with the online space in the period leading up to the election becoming mired in 'personal attacks, fear-driven messaging, and fake narratives targeted [the eventual elected candidate] Nicușor Dan', much of which was fuelled by AI (Radu, 2025). As Roxana Radu puts it, '[w]hile Dan's victory signals resilience in the face of digital manipulation, it also reflects a broader protest vote – a desire to move past the political paralysis and digital toxicity that defined the last six months'

[17] For a different approach, China's Interim Administrative Measures for Generative AI Services and Notice on Issuing 'Measures for the Identification of Artificial Intelligence-Generated Synthetic Content' provide for the labelling of AI-generated content (PWC and Tiang & Partners, 2023; White and Case, 2025). Such labelling laws can arguably (in relatively unintrusive ways) help to protect the electorate against electoral propaganda misinformation and disinformation (see Soon and Quek, 2024).

(Radu, 2025). And, although the DSA represented 'a step in the right direction', the Commission's investigation was 'slow, even for accelerated procedures, like the one opened for the annulled Romanian elections in December 2024', whose conclusions were still awaited in May 2025 (Radu, 2025).

Some legal support for addressing systemic misinformation and disinformation risks in political advertising involving AI systems may also now be found in the EU AI Act's bans on AI practices posing 'unacceptable risks' (article 5), requirements for AI systems classified as high-risk (articles 6 to 15) and labelling *inter alia* of AI-generated deepfake content (article 50). Another potential source of regulation is the EU Regulation on the Transparency and Targeting of Political Advertising 2024 (TTPA) (in effect October 2025). At minimum, this states, political advertising must be labelled and further standards apply for targeting of political advertising online (European Commission, 2025b). Finally worth noting is the increasing use of foreign interference laws *inter alia* to address the problem of 'misinformation and/or disinformation and … foreign intelligence' (Chesterman, 2025: 958).[18]

1.3.4 Scams

In addition to general consumer protections and protections against fraud discussed earlier, scams – or, as Chesterman puts it, 'targeting individuals for the purposes of fraud' – are becoming a focus under the new laws (Chesterman, 2025: 938). For instance, the UK OSA extends to scams as a type of harmful (and illegal) disinformation. Likewise, scam-related disinformation is covered under the EU DSA, and (as noted earlier) the AI Act regulates AI aspects.[19] Australia now has specific far-reaching provisions for scams including in the online environment, with the passing of the Scams Prevention Framework Act 2025 (Cth). Among other things, this empowers the ACCC to 'closely monitor' regulated entities' compliance with Act's 'principles to prevent, detect, disrupt, respond to and report scams', and to enforce the digital platforms sector scams code established under the Act (ACCC, 2022). Singapore also treats scams as a particular

[18] The UK National Security Act of 2023, Singapore Foreign Interference (Countermeasures) Act of 2021 and Australian Foreign Influence Transparency Scheme Act of 2018 are some examples of recent reforms to strengthen the respective jurisdiction's ability to detect and counter foreign interference. See also the US Countering Foreign Propaganda and Disinformation Act (CFPDA) of 2016 and EU TTPA.

[19] But note Recital 29 of the AI Act which states that the AI Act's article 5 prohibitions on AI-enabled manipulative techniques 'are complementary to' the UCPD's provisions (see also Duivenvoorde, 2025).

subject for intervention (Tang, 2025). We have already noted POFMA as a tool to combat online misinformation and disinformation in the public interest, and this applies equally to scams. The Online Criminal Harms Act of 2023 also addresses online scams and obliges online platforms to implement measures to proactively disrupt online scams, including removing scam content upon detection (MDDI, 2024). And Singapore's new Scams Act of 2025 allows *inter alia* for the addressing of scams via restriction orders issued by the police to block credit facilities.

By contrast, in the US efforts to impose obligations on platforms to deal with scams (beyond reliance on the consumer protection provision of the FTCA) would potentially run counter to § 230 CDA, although this may be less so if the platform is viewed as involved in contributing materially to the scam.[20] As to the potential impact of First Amendment when it comes to attempts to regulate scams more generally, as Mark Goodman puts it, although commercial speech and especially false speech is less protected under the First Amendment, '[f]ree speech now means protections sometimes for … scams' (Goodman, 2023; see also Chesterman, 2025: 947 n 83).

1.4 Summary

This section has considered some of the new legislation addressing misinformation and disinformation and their associated harms. As we have seen, there are significant differences between these jurisdictions, with the EU adopting a much more expansive approach in terms of the types of conduct and harms being addressed than the US, and a third group (UK, Australia and Singapore) coming in between. Further, the variations between the jurisdictions surveyed reflect not just different conceptions of what harms should be addressed, and how they should be addressed, but also different balances found with (among other things) freedom of speech and innovation. In particular, the narrow scope of legal regulation of misinformation and disinformation in the US compared to the broader, more open-ended and proactive legal regulation in (most) of the other jurisdictions surveyed, and especially the EU, suggest some very different balances between freedom of speech and innovations in these jurisdictions. This conclusion is reinforced by the recent publication of the US (Republican led) House of Representatives Staff Report characterising the EU DSA as a 'powerful censorship law'

[20] As to which, see *Forrest* v *Meta Platforms, Inc* (2024) (holding that the Meta's § *230* defence failed in a case where the plaintiff argued that Meta had contributed materially to cryptocurrency scams on its platform in which Australian mining magnate Andrew Forrest was falsely represented as endorsing the scams, and the California right of publicity and negligence claims could go forward).

(US Judiciary Committee Staff Report, 2025: 2, 15).[21] While this may be regarded as an extreme statement of the US position on freedom of speech and innovation, there can be little doubt that (as Chesterman puts it) the US 'is somewhat of an outlier in this area, with strong First Amendment protections covering speech that would be unlawful in many other jurisdictions' (Chesterman, 2025: 947, footnote 83).

Such divisions discussed earlier suggest that much of the work in addressing the harms of misinformation and disinformation, which anyway often operate across national and regional boundaries with little regard to law, will (continue to) fall to platforms and their practices, including their uses of technologies, and to broader social measures. Indeed, in our view, one of the strengths of the EU DSA, as explored further in the following section, is its acknowledgement of the value of these alternative modalities.

2 Platforms Using Technologies

2.1 Content Moderation

As our previous section has shown, despite the extensive and highly variable amount of legal regulation focussed on addressing harmful misinformation and disinformation in many jurisdictions, which may be underpinned by different conceptions of rights, there are normative and practical limits to legal intervention. Further, even where there are laws in place, the scale and scope of online content distribution has meant that jurisdictions are increasingly turning to self-regulatory or co-regulatory frameworks that necessarily require the assistance and input of platforms. As a result, it is impossible to discuss the current state of misinformation and disinformation regulation without considering the complex and often-technical system of content moderation that shapes our contemporary online environment. Indeed, one thing that is particularly notable about content moderation today is the way that AI is being employed to detect misinformation and disinformation and suppress its distribution. We outline these developments in this section and highlight an alternative narrative around AI, where the technology is cast as (at least part of) a

[21] Contrast the European Commission which characterises the DSA as required by the EU Charter and 'an important step in defending European values in the online space' (EC, 2024). Likewise, in response to US government and business critiques of the EU AI Act as overly prescriptive, Commission spokesman Thomas Regnier said that, although implementation of some aspects may be delayed, the Commission would 'always remain fully behind the AI Act and its objectives' (Rankin, 2025).

solution to the misinformation and disinformation problem as opposed to the cause. While we are equally sceptical of claims that AI can solve all of these challenges, a claim often circulated by self-interested platforms, our examples allow us to assess the extent to which developments around AI can help address a significant policy issue.

The section also examines key normative questions about the challenges associated with private regulation of speech, in particular deploying technical systems, sometimes in conjunction with human fact-checkers. Of course, the absence of law does not entail the absence of regulation or intervention. And nor does the presence of law necessarily determine the amount of regulation that goes on. It is quite commonly being done privately on platforms anyway, with much less accountability and oversight – although Meta's Oversight Board presents a notable exception here. While this argument about lack of accountability and insight has been made many times (Balkin, 2018; Gillespie, 2018b), we have chosen to highlight Michael Davis, a scholar and former public servant who was involved in the development of Australia's self-regulatory framework around misinformation and disinformation. He notes that without establishing wider regulatory infrastructures, content moderation is left to platforms who become 'the arbiters of truth' (Davis, 2024). We build on this useful critique and suggest that in many cases, these tensions around regulation point to the need for a more sophisticated infrastructure around platforms, involving efforts such as researcher data access and platform observation.

The section proceeds as follows. First, we introduce and define what we mean by content moderation. In the process, we sketch out how AI and other technologies such as blockchain are being deployed by platforms. Second, looking forward, we discuss experimental and scholarly work directed at the capacity of these technologies to detect or address harmful misinformation and disinformation, either by themselves or in conjunction with human fact-checkers – using examples of detecting deepfakes and automated fact-checking to further explore the interventions. Finally, we end with a reflection and development of our argument, addressing what we set out at the beginning of this Element, as well as those views outlined in this section.

2.2 Definitions, Tools and Techniques

The term content moderation refers to a range of practices that digital platforms employ to manage the constant stream of messages, pictures, videos, articles and other forms of content that are published online along with any interactions that occur. One of the most productive and expansive definitions of the term is provided by Gillespie et al. (2020) who describe it as:

> [T]the detection of, assessment of, and interventions taken on content or behaviour deemed unacceptable by platforms or other information intermediaries, including the rules they impose, the human labour and technologies required, and the institutional mechanisms of adjudication, enforcement, and appeal that support it.

From the earlier description, the centrality of private power is made clear. The practice of content moderation emerges from and is shaped by the terms and conditions of platforms as well as any associated guidelines (although legislation can inform these rules). There is also a brief nod to the significant emotional and physical labour that moderation can involve, given its reliance on human beings as well as technical systems (Gillespie, 2018a; Roberts, 2019). While promotion of safety, or alleviation of harm, emerges as an obvious lens through which to view moderation, it is deployed for a range of reasons including managing the spread of misinformation and disinformation. A range of techniques are used to moderate content, and it is worthwhile briefly noting these before turning our focus to the (seemingly) cutting-edge misinformation and disinformation detection technologies promoted as part of the wider AI moment.

Even though the entire goal of content moderation is to anticipate issues and remove problematic content before it is even published on the platform, the large volumes of content posted online every day inevitably continues to cause concern amongst audiences. In response, people are encouraged to 'flag' content that concerns them, which refers to the act of a person using platform tools to report content through the 'predetermined rubric of a platform's [...] community guidelines' (Crawford and Gillespie, 2016: 411). The practice on its own raises significant concerns as people can use the tool to silence or harass 'users that are already vulnerable to platforms' censorship, such as sex workers, LGBTQIA+ and sex-positive users, activists and journalists' (Are, 2024) – to highlight just a few affected demographics.

Another strategy is labelling, which sees potentially controversial or inaccurate content identified as such. In some cases, this may be a fact-check (more on this aspect later), but labels can also include 'a click-through barrier that provides a warning, a content sensitivity alert, or the provision of additional contextual information' (Morrow et al., 2022: 1365). One example of the latter is the addition of a 'forwarded' label on

WhatsApp messages, in an effort to add further context around viral misinformation or spam (Morrow et al., 2022). X (formerly Twitter) also may label content that is 'significantly and deceptively altered, manipulated, or "fabricated"' (Authenticity, 2025). Other digital platforms such as Meta, TikTok and YouTube require users to label AI-generated and manipulated content. There are also growing plans to incorporate content credentials (i.e., metadata that are cryptographically attached to digital content to provide verifiable trails of the content's origins and edits) on their platforms (Soon and Quek, 2024). C2PA is the most visible initiative with a range of key players, from Adobe and Microsoft to BBC and Sony. Other efforts include Open AI ensuring that images generated by their DALL-E 3 model contain metadata. These efforts go beyond classic concerns associated with content moderation and highlight an emerging problem space around ensuring the provenance of content and identifying the presence of synthetic media (Soon and Quek, 2024). While labelling for different purposes has become more prominent across a variety of platforms, the overall efficacy of the intervention is still uncertain (Morrow et al., 2022; Peters, 2023). Still, it presents a potentially useful first step to addressing harms.

Labels do not happen in isolation, with various platforms often seeking to additionally reduce the visibility of labelled content amongst the wider audience. While removal had long been seen as the preferred outcome from content moderation efforts, there are increasing concerns about the potential for 'backfire effects' (Nyhan and Reifler, 2010) where motivated users posting and sharing misinformation become emboldened because of enforcement efforts, which to the targeted individual can feel like censorship. In response to this, platforms are starting to restrict the circulation of suspect content (often called 'borderline content') without removing it from the platform (Gillespie, 2022; Zeng and Kaye, 2022; Are, 2024). The removal of, or restriction of access to, content identified to be false, altered, unverified or harmful, or user accounts propagating such content by digital platforms such as TikTok, Meta and YouTube is arguably done in pursuit of the goal of responsive protection (Soon and Quek, 2024). Once again, these efforts do not always solely focus on issues such as misinformation and disinformation. For example, the approach has allegedly been used by TikTok to restrict the visibility of certain types of content related to the Black Lives Matter movement, developmental disorders (such as autism) and unattractive individuals (Zeng and Kaye, 2022). Along with these efforts, platforms may stop people from engaging with selected content, or creators from monetising their content by, for example, placing advertisements against their posts. With creators rarely told about these interventions, the term 'shadow-banning' (or reduction) has become a commonly used term to describe this form of moderation (Gillespie, 2022; Are, 2024).

Indeed, once we get past interventions like flagging that involve human effort, technical systems and interventions that are commonly referred to as AI starts to enter the picture. Machine learning systems are regularly used to support the shadow-banning (or reduction) methods described previously. The effort involves the use of natural language processing, which relies on supervised training, clean datasets and structured systems to produce predictions. We outline these details to point out the differences between these carefully constructed models, as well as the open and adaptive nature of generative systems like ChatGPT. As Robert Gorwa and colleagues go on to explain, these systems can be used to 'predict whether text may constitute hate speech, and based on that score, flag it for human review' (Gorwa, Binns and Katzenbach, 2020). In a similar fashion, misinformation and disinformation can be identified by using machine learning to extrapolate from a massive database of ratings produced by human classifiers (Gillespie, 2022).

In general, content moderation has always involved the use of technical systems to a greater or lesser extent. The introduction of machine learning has simply resulted in different technical capabilities being made available to both platforms and the human moderators, who are still deeply involved in the overall enterprise. Given this track record, it is perhaps no surprise that one of the most human-intensive misinformation and disinformation interventions – fact-checking, which requires working fact-checkers to develop detailed assessments of incorrect information – is starting to engage with AI technologies. Various platforms collaborate with fact-checking organisations to better identify and correct misinformation and disinformation. Google and YouTube have provided funding to the International Fact-Checking Network to 'increase the impact of fact-checking journalism', and Meta famously introduced a third-party fact-checking programme, which has funded a significant number of fact-checking institutions currently in operation (Watt, Montaña-Niño and Riedlinger, 2025). The most notable deployment was around COVID-19, which saw concerns about the quality of information circulating online become particularly pressing. Conspiracies about how the virus is transmitted, as well as the quality and efficacy of the vaccines, spread like wildfire – in response, platforms were pressured to ensure that official communications were prioritised. Extra initiatives were taken by platforms, demonstrating their stronger commitment to combat misinformation and disinformation over the pandemic, as well as their support of the vaccination programmes (Tan, 2022a, 2022b). For example, both platforms X and Google worked with public health authorities like WHO and the respective health ministries in many countries to review health information on the pandemic and to ensure that credible information is accessible.

Looking forward, there is an increasing perception in technology quarters that some elements of fact-checking – although perhaps not the whole role – may be able to be automated using AI. This raises the following questions: How close are we to a world where 'corrections' are automated, and what are the ethical limitations of moving to this approach?

2.3 From Fact-Checkers to Fact-Bots?

Fact-checking originally started in the early 2000s as a way of correcting the record in political debate, challenging the wordsmithing and obfuscations of statements and claims made by politicians. These efforts were originally located on dedicated websites like FactCheck.org, before gradually spreading across the wider institution of journalism. Various established newsrooms launched their own fact-checking operations, often for election periods; new fact-checking organisations started to appear across the world, with a particular boom period noted in the early to mid-2010s (Graves, 2018; Vinhas and Bastos, 2023). Funding and support for the practice boomed following the election of Donald Trump in 2016. Not only did Trump make a habit of verbally disparaging the press and making wild and inaccurate claims, but as noted earlier, there was evidence of Russian interference in that US election. As part of this period of growth and transition, fact-checking became embedded in the wider content moderation process across various platforms (Vinhas and Bastos, 2023).

It is worth repeating that fact-checking is not (and has never been) wholly free from automation, AI or other technical advances. To pick one leading example from the technology sector, Meta's third-party fact-checking programme, which has been switched to a 'community notes' system in the US,[22] embeds fact-checkers in systems and processes. The standard process involves human fact-checkers accessing a stream of content that Meta's system has identified as misinformation and disinformation. Accredited fact-checking organisations then selected pieces of

[22] Meta in January 2025 announced that it was ending the fact-checking programme in the US and is replacing it with a community-driven system known as 'community notes' on their platforms (i.e., Facebook, Instagram and Threads) instead, stating that this is in prioritisation of free speech and to reduce perceived bias in content moderation.

content to fact-check, and label the content accordingly as 'false, altered or partly false' or 'Missing context' (Meta, 2025). As an interesting aside, the organisations earn revenue from Meta for the completed tasks, which has turned the technology giant into one of the major funders of fact-checking more generally (Watt, Montaña-Niño and Riedlinger, 2025).

Nevertheless, as with many other sectors, questions are being raised about whether human labour can be augmented (or even replaced) with AI. Fact-checking – like all journalism – takes a significant amount of time. Phone calls need to be made, information must be sourced, and details must be confirmed and re-confirmed before publication. The question is whether automation and AI can help do this within a shorter time and at lower costs. Many platforms are relying on algorithmic moderation and promoting authoritative sources, rather than deleting misinformation which could reflect alternative viewpoints or constitute legitimate dissent. As a result, these platforms are making certain disputable or contestable content less visible, rather than removing it completely, hence allowing for different perspectives to be shared while reducing the viral potential of what could be harmful falsehoods (see Cademix, 2025).

Discussions around efficiencies are a common feature of debates around AI and the labour market, and it is no surprise that we find them circulating around fact-checking (OECD, 2021). For one, these tendencies align with the natural philosophical orientation of technology firms raised in the ashes of the 'Californian ideology' (Barbrook and Cameron, 1996) – one centred around optimism and technological determinism – to embrace technical solutions over socio-technical interventions. However, the sort of policy discourses we set out in the opening of this Element have also added to the perceived sense of crisis and the need for automation. If there is a misinformation and disinformation crisis on our hands, and Generative AI is going to lead to even more error-strewn or conspiratorial information circulating online, then an argument can be easily made that these issues are no longer able to be managed by purely human interventions. These fact-checking specific debates also fit into a much a wider narrative around content moderation and scale (Gillespie, 2020) which both invokes and demands AI and automation as some sort of solution to managing the significant amount of content online. Early evidence, however, reveals that AI is being used increasingly as a way of augmenting fact-checking work, rather than replacing it entirely.

Critical work is still being done in universities, with researchers actively experimenting with technology to better understand how AI can assist fact-checkers. In a literature review on what they call automated fact-checking

(AFC), Dierickx and colleagues (2023) identify four different areas where AFC may be valuable: finding claims, detecting already fact-checked claims, evidence retrieval and verification. Guo and colleagues (2022) offer a broadly similar framework but go further in outlining the specific technologies involved. For example, they describe the growing use of neural networks to help identify whether a particular claim is worth checking. The ability to incorporate additional context around the claim is incredibly beneficial, when compared to previous classification efforts which had to rely on fixed features, such as up-votes or named political entities such as parties or politicians. Other efforts have seen LLMs increasingly used to identify the veracity of certain claims. However, because AI systems are dependent on the datasets upon which they are trained – a phrase which has become something of a truism in recent years – the ability of AI to detect false information may be limited.

For the success of these systems, what is considered to be misinformation and disinformation to be censored must be agreed on. One significant shortcoming is the over-blocking of lawful content by AI through its over-inclusivity, henceforth potentially negatively affecting the freedom of expression through censorship of reliable content (Kertysova, 2018). In the same vein, the systems also appear to be inaccurate, with Das and colleagues (2023) noting that 'even the state-of-the-art natural language processing models perform poorly on [...] benchmarks', referring to the capacity of models to accurately detect claims worth checking.

Although the deployment of automation including especially AI in the context of fact-checking is still in its infancy, there is a growing effort to use the technology to assist both content moderation directly, as well as support downstream efforts in fact-checking organisations. As might be expected, the other area where AI is being deployed with a view to supporting content moderation in the future is in relation to deepfakes, where a similar tale of experimental academic research and gradual industry engagement is occurring. Both of these examples are discussed further in the following section.

2.3.1 Detecting Deepfakes

Certain sub-disciplines in computer science have started to focus some of their efforts on the detection of deepfakes with the support of industry. Meta ran a Deepfake Detection Challenge in 2019, and Google has released a dataset of deepfake videos to support research efforts in the field (Meta, 2020; Dufour and Gully, 2019). Platforms are also keen to promote their detection abilities across their products, with Meta changing their Facebook policies in preparation for the US election, going so far as to label 'digitally altered media' that was likely to have an impact on the public's interpretation of the campaign (Paul, 2024). The way that technology companies communicate about these initiatives can imply that deepfake detection is a solved problem, and something that can easily be incorporated into existing content moderation routines. However, the technical capacity to detect manipulated media is still developing with efforts directed to improve state of the art methods.

Before exploring the process of deepfake detection, it is worth talking about exactly what AI manipulation looks like. As we already know, deepfakes can be image, video or audio based and can be deployed in several ways. For example, an audio deepfake might get a celebrity voice to conform to a particular script or alternatively, prerecorded audio might be amended to sound more like the celebrity (Patel et al., 2023). Similarly, an image might be entirely AI-generated or combine two or more photos into a new context. These descriptions are really scene-setting – what is most critical for detection is understanding minor changes that can still be discernible. For example, if the lighting in a static image is changed, detection might involve 'analysing the image's metadata [or] searching for inconsistencies in the image's pixels or patterns' (Kaur et al., 2024). With videos, it can be more productive to look for 'visible inconsistencies', such as an 'inconsistent head pose' or a strange 'blinking pattern' (Patel et al., 2023).

Some of these identification methods can be achieved through a dedicated visual check or through basic open-source tools, that support operations like metadata analysis. However, the vast majority of deepfake detection methods rely on AI – and more specifically deep learning – for reasons of scale and efficiency. Like most forms of deep learning, this involves training an AI model on datasets to identify 'patterns, anomalies, or inconsistencies' through statistical analysis, prediction and identification (Kaur et al., 2024). The dataset used by Facebook's Deepfake Detection Challenge provides some insight into the scale and type of data being used by these models. It contained '128,154 videos sourced from 3,426 paid actors' and featured '104,500 fake and 23,654 real videos', with videos recorded in various lighting conditions (Stroebel et al., 2023). A research team would build a model to be trained on this dataset (or perhaps another one), and then focus on statistically identifying inconsistencies or errors. While we have already noted some, a particularly fascinating example comes from Agarwal and colleagues, who have found that deepfake videos do not effectively reproduce mouth shapes (or visemes). While the mouth should completely close to pronounce words using the letters M, B and P, this does not happen in deepfake videos. To address this issue, they trained a neural network to identify whether 'a mouth is open or closed in a single video frame' (Agarwal et al., 2020). Additional complications are presented by developments in synthetic imagery. It is important to note that the tools mentioned earlier were already struggling with simple face swaps, and synthetic media has developed significantly since then.

Available deep learning models perform well on the datasets they are trained on, but there is still a difference between what success looks like and the realities of content moderation. The winner of the Deepfake Detection Challenge won with an accuracy of 82.56% – while impressive, this still represents an almost 20% error rate. Indeed, although various detection models function reasonably well on the datasets they are trained on, they still perform poorly in the wild, when assessing deepfakes they have not come across before (Kaur et al., 2024). For example, the winning Detection Challenge model's success rate went down to 65.18% when tested against a black box dataset (a dataset where no-one knows what's in it). As a result, as Stroebel and colleagues note, while these models report 'high performances in these metrics when trained, validated, and tested on the same dataset', they are not generalisable, and therefore are not 'equipped to handle real-world applications' (Stroebel et al., 2023).

There are also adjacent challenges associated with computational resources and diversity. On the first issue, developing increasingly complex models in the search for accuracy can be beneficial from a technical perspective, but little consideration is given to the length of time associated with deepfake detection (Kaur et al., 2024). A balance between accuracy and efficiency will need to be achieved before any detection systems can be integrated into existing content moderation systems. On the topic of diversity, dataset availability and composition remain a critical issue with respect to detection. There can be significant shortfalls of key demographics in available visual datasets, which has led to the introduction of specific datasets to address the issue, like the Korean Deepfake Detection Dataset to improve knowledge of Asian facial features. However, some other notable gaps remain, like the 'limited amount of available full-body deepfake data' (Edwards et al., 2024). There is also a continuing focus on visual deepfakes, whether they be image or video, with a noticeable absence of studies looking at synthetic audio (Stroebel et al., 2023). When audio deepfakes are considered, the vast majority of studies focus on the English language (Dixit, Kaur and Kingra, 2023).

2.3.2 Automated Fact-Checking

Looking beyond deepfake detection, we are also seeing evidence of augmentation with AI tools in automated fact-checking practice. US-based fact-checking unit, PolitiFact, 'uses a large database of claims, called ClaimReview, to detect what a politician says in a video, match it to a previously published fact-check, and display the relevant fact-check onscreen'. While the process is not without error, Professor Bill Adair – the founder of the organisation – describes the benefits of 'instant fact-checking' (Abels, 2022). Snopes have developed a chatbot, establishing a large language model based on their archives, which allows people to ask questions about rumours (Richmond, 2024).

Deepfake detection can be said to be less progressed than automated fact-checking, with limited incorporation into existing content moderation efforts. That being said, these trends do collectively point to something of an arms race, with various AI capacities being developed in response to an anticipated increase in misinformation and disinformation.

2.4 Technical and Ethical Limitations

As mentioned earlier, AI systems are technically dependent on the datasets upon which they are trained, and its capabilities in detecting false information can be limited. Hence, it becomes imperative for the training dataset: to be large enough so that it can be adequately reflective for the AI to differentiate between false information and truth; to be updated regularly to counter new campaigns; and to contain text accurately labelled as false content (Marsoof et al., 2023). Ascertaining which content is false can be hard, since online content may contain a mix of true, false, as well as true but misleading claims. Further, there may be opinions, speculations and predictions not intended by the author to be assertions of fact. These subtle differences both between what is true and what is false or misleading, as well as what are opinions and facts can only be identified with linguistic competence and background knowledge of more complex topics (Brasoveanu and Andonie, 2021), which trained AI may not have at hand. Prior studies have also demonstrated that reliably labelled datasets of false information are hard to come by (Asr and Toboada, 2019). Therefore, notwithstanding the promise of automated techniques, algorithmic moderation has the potential to exacerbate, rather than relieve, several key problems with content policy.

There are several tensions that need to be resolved. For example, when the removal of content by a 'fallible' human moderator is associated with scientific impartiality, it allows online platforms to both justify replacing people with automated systems as well as keep their decisions non-negotiable and non-transparent (Crawford, 2016). This worsens the problem that content moderation is infamously seen to be an opaque and secretive process (Gillespie, 2018b; Flew, Suzor and Martin, 2019). The absence of a human-in-the-loop in fully automated decision-making systems is a dangerous progression. To elaborate on what has been said earlier, because machine learning is notoriously poor at making difficult context-dependent decisions, automated systems could *both over-block* important forms of expression, or *under-block* such content (including harmful content), thereby not protecting informational integrity either way. Having people in the loop moderates this risk and limitation of AI. As algorithmic moderation becomes more seamlessly integrated into regular users' daily online experience, the reality behind the use of automated decision making in content moderation must continue to be questioned, so that online platforms remain accountable to the public and engaged with crucial content policy decisions (Gorwa, Binns and Katzenbach, 2020).

Unfortunately, some AI systems like large language models are unexplainable (or at least very difficult to explain), involving sophisticated layers of architecture that are almost impossible to analyse and explain – they are hence frequently referred to as 'black boxes' as there is little insight into how they are coded, what datasets they are trained on, how they identify co-relations and make decisions, as well as how accurate and reliable they are (Pasquale, 2025a). If users do not understand why their content is removed due to the lack of transparency, accountability and explainability in platforms' content moderation policies, their trust in online platforms may be eroded, together with their ability to challenge takedowns, thereby impacting on these users' rights to online speech (Fischman-Afori, 2023; Marsoof et al., 2023). It has been suggested that some implementations of algorithmic moderation techniques threaten to: decrease decisional transparency, through making non-transparent practices even more difficult to understand; complicate outstanding issues of justice (with respect to biases and how certain viewpoints, groups or types of speech are privileged); as well as obscure the complex politics that underlie the practices of contemporary content platform moderation (Gorwa, Binns and Katzenbach, 2020). Given these critiques it has been suggested that the use of content-filtering AI should always be subject to mandatory human review (i.e. a human-in-the-loop), particularly in high-risk and low-accuracy scenarios (Marsoof et al., 2023). And, to further improve accuracy, datasets relied on to train such AI should contain articles which are individually labelled by people with expertise on the topic of these articles (Asr and Toboada, 2019).

Digital platforms are making some efforts to improve the accuracy of AI systems. For instance, platforms like YouTube are partnering with external evaluators and using their inputs as training data for machine learning systems to build models that review large volumes of videos to detect harmful misinformation and disinformation. OpenAI has been working on developing detection classifiers to evaluate the likelihood that the content is AI generated (Soon and Quek, 2024). Additionally, given the challenges of AI-based systems in understanding subtler forms of human expression and contextual cues beyond explicit content, such as sarcasm and irony that can give content further meaning (Santos, 2023), the approach of semi-supervised learning – involving people in the text analysis process to develop AI tools for the automated detection of misinformation and disinformation – may ameliorate these difficulties and further help to improve the accuracy of such tools. Similarly, involving people in the *actual* detection of misinformation and disinformation may circumvent the challenges faced with respect to the accuracy of textual analysis programmes in identifying misinformation and disinformation, due to the difficulty of parsing complex and sometimes conflicting meanings from text (Marsden and Meyer, 2019).

Additionally, while no longer seen as especially viable, blockchain technology has also been considered as a method of verifying the authenticity of digital content. Blockchains can provide a transparent and immutable record of authenticity. Examples of initiatives that use blockchain to combat misinformation and disinformation include the News Provenance Project, Fake Check and Democracy Notary. The New York Times, for instance, conducted a project to provide provenance metadata around news, using blockchain technology to track the dissemination and provide contextual information to readers of online news (Santos, 2023). Separately, there are initiatives such as the DeepTrust Alliance which verifies the provenance and authenticity of digital content (through metadata), as well as WeVerify's Deepfake Detector which maintains a public database of known fakes and uses blockchain to scrutinise social media and web content for disinformation and fabricated content (Harrison and

Leopold, 2021). As Fátima Santos concludes after an exhaustive study, combining blockchain technologies with AI's capacity to analyse large volumes of content in real time can result in a more efficient system against misinformation and disinformation (Santos, 2023). At the same time, she does not suggest that these tools can provide a complete solution, arguing rather that 'the fight against disinformation requires a multifaceted approach that involves not only the use of AI and other technological tools but also human verification'.

2.5 Value and Limits of Technical Regulation

There are ongoing normative debates about the role that private entities should play in the regulation of private speech (Klonick, 2017; Balkin, 2018; Gillespie, 2018a; Santos, 2023). As Davis and Molitorisz put it (2025: 3), 'platforms are largely to control the dissemination of content on their services, and this lies at the heart of their market offering [...] and their moderation of content often exhibits arbitrariness, inconsistency and deference to power rather than rights'. While we have been emphasising the tools available to platforms to address misinformation and disinformation in this section, our comments highlight the limits of leaving the choice whether to do so, or not, to private actors – whose practices may vary sharply, shaped by corporate goals of maximising user engagement and profit *or* political changes, and whose ideas about what and how misinformation and disinformation should be regulated may also be very different from those of their own communities.[23] Indeed, even where decisions made by platforms seek to address misinformation and disinformation, technical tools may still be insufficient, especially if the end goal is alleviation of harm and/or vindication of some idea of rights. They may also be controversial. For instance, the use of AI and technological tools in fact-checking and content moderation processes often face technical and ethical challenges.

The question we now turn to is whether, given our arguments that reliance on law, and even platforms and their technologies will not be enough to address the harmful effects of misinformation and disinformation in balance with freedom of speech and innovation, social interventions can assist.

[23] Compare Chesterman, a notable legal defender of the use of AI systems in regulation who concludes that legitimacy and efficacy will be greatest 'when endorsed by publicly accountable [human] institutions' whose work is centred on serving 'we the peoples' (Chesterman, 2021: 5, 246).

3 Building Social Resilience

3.1 Beyond Law and Technology

In this section we outline the important role of tools and approaches which are predominantly social. We are mindful not just of the harms which are already being identified with misinformation and disinformation, including those being targeted by various laws (as discussed in Section 1) or highlighted in the moderation of platforms (as discussed in Section 2), but the need to build general social resilience so as better to head off future harms. The idea that tackling misinformation and disinformation for the future requires 'a comprehensive or total defence system, in which every individual and organisation should play a role, including as checks and balances in the overall information ecosystem' is not a new idea (see, e.g., OECD 2024: 74). But what is needed is a fuller understanding of the predominantly social tools and approaches that might be adopted within that system.

It is important also to set out exactly what we mean here. Some legal frameworks have avenues for ordinary people to activate, or even participate in, certain processes. For example, under the EU DSA (discussed in Section 1) people are empowered to flag illegal content on platforms under (article 16), have recourse to an internal complaint handling system that providers of platforms must provide (article 20) and can escalate unresolved complaints to an independent settlement body (article 21). In addition, there is scope for civil society groups such as fact-checkers or other NGOs to be identified as trusted flaggers with their notices 'given priority [...] processed and decided upon without undue delay' (article 22(1)). And vetted researchers may be granted access to conduct research 'that contributes to the detection, identification and understanding of systemic risks' (article 40(4)). Platforms, which are required to conduct risk assessment and mitigation, are also encouraged to include input from communities (and the European Commission conducts its own consultation: see Jahangir, 2025a). In this respect, EU law is very different from the law in the US, for instance. But such approaches offer a useful way of incorporating wider society into legal responses, ensuring that a range of actors are involved in platform governance.

However, there are some harms that are not easily accounted for by legal frameworks or technological solutions. One challenge that some scholars have begun pointing to already is the 'foundational' problem of people (individually and collectively) not knowing when to believe and when not to believe in the truth of information being circulated and the resultant lack of trust in all information (see Jungherr, 2024). For instance, writing in 2019, Robert Chesney and Danielle Citron posited that the perverse product of such an environment where this phenomenon becomes widespread is the 'liar's dividend' – here, the public dismisses genuine allegations of wrongdoing because the basis of truth has become muddled with that of falsity (Chesney and Citron, 2019). More recently, Chesterman argues that the harm here may not (just) be that people believe in lies, but that they cease to believe in anything at all (Chesterman, 2025). Frank Pasquale suggests further that people may become demoralised, and hence too cynical or disengaged to participate in democracy (Pasquale, 2025b; cf. also Philip, 2020; Kreps and Kriner, 2023). At present this nebulous 'harm' arguably finds little support in current ethical standards and declarations of rights (although see Pasquale, 2025b, advocating for a 'maximalist' conception of rights). However, it is one that we believe will ultimately demand considered attention from policymakers and society more generally.

Below we detail more systemic social approaches to combatting misinformation and disinformation, including extending the role for trusted third parties to monitor and address harms, building digital literacy, and making space for continuing further research (including on the scale of the problem, the immediate and more fundamental harms that need to be addressed, and measures that may effectively address these without undermining freedom of speech). In our proposals we identify two features that we think are important guiding principles: first, a move away from the idea that contesting truth and falsity is the best way to deal with misinformation and disinformation instead centring on harm as the justification for intervention; and, second, devising an approach which is genuinely social and geared to communities rather than just relying on experts and elites to lead the way.

3.2 Devising Social Solutions

As we have already seen, third parties have emerged to battle misinformation and disinformation. Changes include the rapid growth in the fact-checking industry, as a way for digital platforms to help outsource their content moderation challenges, and journalists to reclaim their role as arbiters and authorities of establishing the truth of current events (Graves, 2018; Cotter, DeCook and Kanthawala, 2022). Alongside professional fact-checkers, community volunteers have been deployed by platforms X and Meta and introduced by YouTube. These volunteers may make a useful contribution to reliable information as shown by the experience of Wikipedia (Tkacz, 2014).[24] Scholars have raised concerns that a community notes system could miss falsehoods and amplify hateful content (see Gilbert, 2025), but there is some evidence that community notes are viewed as more trustworthy than expert-tagged misinformation flags (Drolsbach, Solovev and Prollochs, 2024). Moreover, John Wihbey points to another benefit of community notes functioning as '"bridging" mechanisms that funnel disparate people together into more deliberative and cooperative tasks of producing counterspeech together' (Wihbey, 2025b: 75).

A body of evidence is also emerging to suggest that community notes work best on platforms in tandem with professional fact-checking. Through this partnership notes can appear faster on misleading posts, henceforth allowing misinformation and disinformation to be addressed before it spreads further (Nyariki, 2025). While fact-checking has continued to struggle with combatting the spread of misinformation and disinformation on platforms, these collaborations suggest a promising way forward.

There are potential limits to the effectiveness of community notes though. Recent research has found that people who look to social media and commercial broadcasting (i.e., television or radio) for information, score lower on a civic values scale, than those who turn to newspapers, online news aggregators and non-commercial television. The scale measures the levels of trust in media institutions and the government, as well as people's openness to considering perspectives that challenge their own (Andrejevic, 2025).[25] As a result, while community notes may be seen as trustworthy by the public and even help fact-checkers, their effectiveness could be limited by the civic dispositions of the media audiences who are likely to be involved in the effort.

What then of platforms delegating responsibilities regarding content moderation to trusted entities? We have noted earlier the role of trusted professional fact-checkers supplementing (and acting as a check on) the activities of community actors. But also consider here the role of trusted entities which serve as dispute resolvers when platform content moderation decisions are challenged. Kate Klonick (2017) points to Meta (previously

[24] The Wikipedia model, for example, arguably provides a positive historical example of relying on community notes.

[25] Andrejevic reports on a survey of 2,046 Australians conducted with Essential Media which found that people who relied on social media and commercial broadcasting (i.e., television or radio) scored significantly lower on a civic values scale than those who relied on newspapers, online news aggregators and non-commercial television (Andrejevic, 2025).

Facebook) as having taken meaningful steps towards redressing issues through the development and launch of its Oversight Board, which enables user participation and offers something close to procedural fairness (Klonick, 2020). Further, the Oversight Board's reliance on the international human rights standards of the United Nations' International Covenant on Civil and Political Rights (1966) offers the promise of an international set of norms about fundamental rights (rather than privileging, for instance, US ideas about the overriding importance of free speech or European ideas about the need to vigorously regulate hate speech).

Could more be done to integrate the work of the Oversight Board's experts with the broader community? As Evelyn Douek points out, the Oversight Board's 'material impacts' on online speech are hard to track – and in high-profile, especially hard cases, 'the Board has too often ducked its responsibility to act as decider of last resort and avoided giving a definitive answer altogether' (Douek, 2024: 379–80). On the other hand, we might wonder whether the Oversight Board's indecisiveness is a harbinger of hybrid models that bring together experts and communities. In critiquing Oversight Board's indeterminacy, Douek gives the example of the Board's COVID-19 misinformation decision in response to Meta's request for advice in 2022 about 'whether Meta's current measures to address COVID-19 misinformation under [its] harmful health misinformation policy continues to be appropriate' considering the changing pandemic conditions. Its response was to advise Meta to continue its current policy but also begin a process to reassess the health-related claims Meta currently removes, through stake holder engagement. Douek questions here 'wasn't that exactly what Meta was asking the Board to do?' (2024: 432). Yet, as Douek points out, given that COVID-19 misinformation is one of the most politically controversial topics in content moderation, we might see the justification for trying to bring in a range of knowledge and opinions to address the issue, with trusted experts.

A similar response might be offered to proposals from Andrew Kenyon for what he calls greater 'democracy of expression' (Kenyon, 2021; and see also Kenyon, 2024), emphasising diversity of speech as a key to countering misinformation and disinformation. As Ian Cram argues, by excluding all but the rational, consensus-seeking and civilised speech, little contentious discourse will be let in (Cram, 2019: 140). Kenyon further argues that 'trusted public media' should be able to be relied on to counter potential misinformation and disinformation with other reliable information, giving the examples of German and French public media (Kenyon, 2021: 241).

However, we might wonder whether public media are necessarily well placed to carry out this role if operating independently of communities they serve.[26] Could diverse private media and community media – if found sufficiently credible by community standards – help to make up the difference?

On the one hand, both media play a particularly critical role when it comes to the amplification of misinformation and disinformation. Work by Axel Bruns and colleagues show how conspiracy claims associated with the spread of COVID-19 were amplified by mainstream media reportage (Bruns, Harrington and Hurcombe, 2021). These views were largely shared within existing conspiracist networks until celebrities started to make similar claims, resulting in news and entertainment outlets reporting on the controversial opinions of the rich and famous. Reporting was led by 'entertainment news outlets, and entertainment journalists within larger news organisations', with stories adopting 'an amused or dismissive tone' rather than challenging the claims being made. On the other hand, statistical studies lead by Sacha Altay (Altay, Nielsen and Fletcher, 2024) show that, in general, mainstream media news consumption correlates with a stronger awareness of false or contestable claims, and a lower susceptibility to embracing these by news consumers. In our view, these studies can sit in productive tension with one another. While we might view ongoing engagement with news as a useful balance to false beliefs (Altay, Nielsen and Fletcher, 2024), media amplification of misinformation and disinformation still matters because we cannot expect all individuals to be regular, engaged news consumers. In that context, responsible reporting becomes key as a socially oriented solution, necessarily involving ongoing engagement with experts and communities if conspiracist claims are to be effectively challenged.

One option to support this kind of work might be to consider greater engagement with community-oriented mechanisms that have historically helped to build institutional trust, such as newspaper readers' editors or ombudsmen. These were roles that either stood in for, advocated for or engaged with the audience, creating a link between the newspaper and the wider community (Ferrucci, 2019). Such positions have been gradually in decline, with reader comments, social media and external media commentary viewed as suitable replacements. While these developments have all been valuable in their own way, they do not offer formal accountability – as

[26] There may also be a question of expertise. The Australian ARC Centre of Excellence for Automated Decision-Making and Society, for instance, highlights that independent fact-checkers play a role in limiting the circulation of misinformation and disinformation, over the general provision of public interest media (Meese et al., 2024).

a result, news outlets have not really availed themselves of the opportunity to both learn from and respond to community concerns, particularly around reporting conspiracies or covering content in a sensationalist or controversial fashion.[27]

Of course, in our discussion of the news media – and particularly private media – we do not seek to diminish the baseline level of journalistic standards that most newsrooms adhere to, or the value of press codes more broadly. These codes can help to establish a reliable media ecosystem and generate an expectation of reliable speech and information. The problem is when institutional positions and self-regulatory instruments get used as proxies for trust rather than reflecting actual behaviour. Questions can be raised about what media do with their legitimacy. How do they handle misinformation and disinformation when it comes to their own reporting practices (as noted by Bruns and colleagues earlier)? Does sensationalism further threaten audience trust? As already discussed, loss of trust can separate the media from the audience quite dramatically. With people in some countries no longer actively consuming news content, maintaining this relationship becomes increasingly critical (Villi et al., 2022). Consequently, the news media are presented with a wider challenge that requires them to look beyond established institutional regulatory patterns and reflect on the critical role they play in a disrupted information ecosystem.

Our earlier examples have shown the limits of institutional capacity and highlight the value of focussing on a rich diversity of civic practices that can contribute to a healthier media ecosystem. Instead of relying (just) on regulatory proxies or formal determinations, the most effective interventions appear to be community led and socially supported. However, this can only occur if audiences have media literacy (see, for instance, Coe, 2023), a topic we now turn to.

3.3 Improving Media and Algorithmic Literacy

Looking to community involvement in solutions, as well as relying on the abilities – and readiness – of audiences to recognise, and presumably then disbelieve, misinformation and disinformation when they come across it requires a degree of media literacy. In addition to efforts at fact-checking and providing alternative sources of information, some institutions are turning to pre-bunking, which involves building up people's media literacy

[27] Although the BBC has had audience councils since the mid-2000s and offers one potential way to better establish a stronger bond between audiences and newsrooms.

skills (Ecker et al., 2022) to increase their resilience to misinformation and disinformation.

There is moderate evidence for the effectiveness of media literacy training (Altay, 2022) and some gamification strategies (Glas et al., 2023; Birrer and Just, 2024), which suggests that wider education strategies may be more beneficial, when anticipating any significant influx of incorrect information emerging from AI-generated or distributed content. There is much work to do here in some countries, with research into Australian educational settings showing that teachers are not well supported to embed media literacy into the curriculum (Corser, Dezuanni and Notley, 2022). However, recent work of the eSafety Commissioner on developing a 'Best Practice Framework' (eSafety Commissioner, 2024) may help to address that deficit. Moreover, progress is being made more generally, for instance in Europe (although with variation: see Pranaityte et al., 2024), in some US states like New Jersey that mandate the teaching of media literacy from K–12 (Burney, 2023), and with a widespread review in the UK suggesting a similar intervention[28] (Badshah, 2024).

It is also important to look beyond the traditional focus on content. A growing number of researchers are highlighting the importance of algorithmic literacy, noting it is increasingly necessary to understand the technical systems and contexts through which content is circulated and promoted. Leyla Dogruel and colleagues (2022) provide a useful working definition, describing it as:

> [B]eing aware of the use of algorithms in online applications, platforms, and services, knowing how algorithms work, being able to critically evaluate algorithmic decision-making as well as having the skills to cope with or even influence algorithmic operations.

They go on to explore literacy rigorously through a validated scale, but literacy can also be spotted more generally, with certain people – such as professional content creators – developing robust 'folk theories' about how certain algorithms work (Dogruel, 2021). This area is still developing though and perhaps in the same space that media literacy was a few decades ago, with approaches and interventions still at a very nascent stage of development (Oeldorf-Hirsch and Neubaum, 2025). That being said, algorithmic literacy is a critical educative step, that may help people

[28] UK's regulator Ofcom is already under a duty, pursuant to section 11 of the Communications Act 2003, to promote media literacy, including to build citizens' resilience to false information.

understand not just how to spot problematic content, but why they came across it in the first place.

Private companies are taking incredibly small steps in this regard. Meta now provides a prompt on its feeds to explain to people why they are seeing certain advertisements. However, research has shown that the feature tends to suggest that targeting occurs through basic category matching rather than by the 'dynamic, associative machine learning process' (Burgess et al., 2024) that drives Meta's infrastructure. The focus on individual targeting also ignores developments in advertising, where an embrace of Generative AI allows advertisements to iterate over time, engaging users effectively through changing in response to user preferences and behaviours (Carah et al., 2024). Similar efforts have been undertaken by TikTok, which provides equally vague insight into its content recommendation processes (Main, 2022). As a result, algorithmic literacy may only be enhanced through empowering individuals and communities to engage with these systems on their terms.

Regardless of whether these reforms eventuate, we believe there is a need to prioritise both media and algorithmic literacy. Leaving aside the challenges around the educational arena, adults also have limited knowledge with respect to media. A 2024 survey conducted by Tanya Notley and colleagues (2024) in Australia have found that less than half of Australian adults are confident that they can check if information found online is true, or if a website can be trusted. More notably, only 33% of Australians feel that they know what media literacy even means (Notley et al., 2024). Similar studies conducted in 2023 by Ofcom in the UK reveal that since 2015 around 40% of respondents over 16 continue to state that they do not critically assess search results, with the overall percentage largely holding steady since then (OFCOM, 2023: 22). Around half the survey population also regularly do not identify or recognise the first few links as sponsored. These studies show that while the use of digital technology is widespread, there are still notable skills gaps around assessing and evaluating information. As noted earlier, this does not mean that people are liable to believe everything they read, but rather that they are clearly uncertain about navigating an increasingly complex information ecosystem.

That being said, while literacy efforts provide general support and protection for the population at large, there is evidence to suggest that these initiatives do not help the small proportion of people who actively seek out misinformation or come across it. A key reason for this lack of efficacy is that in specific contexts (such as politics), people are not motivated by accuracy but are instead seeking to accept information that confirms pre-existing beliefs (Nyhan, 2020). Further insights into the complexity surrounding underlying motivations to access this sort of content were revealed in recent study on conspiracy theories in Australia and New Zealand. Matthew Marques and colleagues (2022) found that a belief in conspiracy theories correlated with relational and existential factors (such as less trust in government and others, as respective examples). However, there was no correlation with critical thinking, which meant that people were not turning to conspiracies to make sense of the world. Corrections or other forms of fact-checking are therefore likely to have a limited impact on these core groups of politically motivated misinformation consumers and conspiracy theorists, who may also be most prone to contribute to harms (Stockemer and Bordeleau, 2024).

In addition to the limited inoculative effect of improving literacy for high-risk populations, more expansive critiques can be made. As the earlier overview reveals, much of literacy discussions are largely focussed on skills, with education programmes in schools easily cast as capacity building interventions. It can be easy to embrace this sort of approach, which promises some sort of broad causal link between news literacy and the spread of misinformation and disinformation. However, notable media literacy practitioner and theorist Paul Mihailidis cautions against this, arguing for initiatives that foster a 'civic intentionality' (Mihailidis, 2018). Instead of stepping away from media and assessing it, he calls for 'interventions [...] designed to bring people together in support of solving social problems, reinventing spaces for meaningful engagement [and] creating positive dialog' (p. 159). These efforts align with our call for a less instrumentalist approach to misinformation and disinformation.

In addition to enabling a range of people (including children, young people and adults of different backgrounds and political persuasions) to better participate and engage in social life, and support a healthier media ecosystem, these social solutions may offer opportunities for conspiracy theorists to reconnect with the mainstream. At very least, there is a case for reaching out to them if only to appreciate what the mainstream is up against and find ways to make their practices more transparent and counteract their influence. For instance, Allan Britton (2025) argues that media literacy programmes can foster diverse viewpoints and mitigate against echo chambers that reinforce conspiratorial beliefs. Of course, the risk is that the publics may come to embrace conspiratorial thinking through these processes. Perhaps, the best we can hope for is that ultimately the social conclusions they draw will come to be seen as wrong with the benefit of experience.

3.4 Making Space for Research

Bernhard Rieder and Jeanette Hoffman (2020) note that platforms are inherent dynamic environments and argue that such 'volatility … requires continuous observation'. Currently, many worries about misinformation and disinformation are anticipatory and speculative. Examples that do exist are often idiosyncratic examples with little context or knowledge provided about wider causal impacts. Even in the case of well-understood harms that relevant communities might agree need to be addressed, at least to some extent, in balance with freedom of speech and innovation, there can be differences at the margins. For example, political interference in elections might be a general social concern but while there is evidence of misinformation and disinformation circulating around elections, we do not always have a sense of its audience, overall impact or the source.

Observation won't help us with all these problems, but it will take us some of the way there, allowing researchers to assess and analyse critical datasets and better understand the current ecosystem (cf. Wihbey, 2025b: 75). Likewise, particular cases where elections were obviously subject to extreme pressure from external actors (as with the Romanian elections of 2024 and 2025 discussed in Section 1.3.3) provide useful case studies for researchers' efforts as well as pointing to the practical need for ongoing sustained research into measures needed to avoid such events in the future. Such efforts are likely to sit productively alongside the sorts of monitoring done by state intelligence of external actors seeking to disrupt electoral processes.

As noted earlier, law can help here (see generally Lessig, 1999, 2006; Tan, 2018). For instance, while article 16 of the EU DSA provides for trusted flaggers to be given priority by platforms within their designated areas of expertise (van de Kerkhof, 2025), article 40 provides for access by vetted researchers who conduct research 'that contributes to the detection, identification and understanding of systemic risks'.[29] However what we are arguing for in this section is participation by researchers at a level going beyond, and in ways that, laws may not easily (or need to) accommodate.

3.5 Enhancing Democracy

Social measures and tools can also act as a counter to the anti-democratic use of technologies (as well as laws). As we have seen whether one automates different elements of a fact-check or detects deepfakes using

[29] Already, X's failure to provide the necessary access to researchers contributed to the European Commission's determination in 2024 that it was in breach of the DSA, with the prospect of a very large fine (exceeding US$ 1 billion) currently in contemplation (Jahangir, 2025b).

machine learning, the technical components rely on natural language processing, statistical modelling and probabilistic labelling to assess textual claims, or convolutional neural networks that can analyse audio and video signals. However, the outcomes from these technologies can be used to justify a normative model of communication and democracy that presumes 'reason, rationality and truth' to quote Johan Farkas and Jannick Schou (2019: 5). Indeed, a narrative that we are contesting in this Element adheres to this presumption, gesturing to an idealised online environment before social media and Generative AI, where truth and falsities were (thought to be) easily identified. Farkas and Schou critique this ongoing focus on truth and in doing so, offer a diagnosis for democracy, arguing that beyond 'facts, reason and evidence', democracies are also about 'giving voice to different political projects and groups' (2019: 7).

Our concerns about democracy are more pragmatic, but no less normative. We suggest that concerns about truth and falsity often sit outside of the embodied, emotional, multi-layered world of actual conspiratorial thinking and disenfranchised people that consume and spread misinformation and disinformation. We are not making claims of relativism here but rather point to ongoing issues associated with seeking to automate truth and veracity, when we are engaging with a deeply emotional terrain where correctness and correction may not even be the right paradigms from which to engage. While we have argued that community input can act as a democratic counter to the content moderation of platforms and technologies, along with (other) elites, a broader perspective would ask whether truth should even be our north star when seeking to address the policy problems at hand. As we are seeing with a range of legal interventions, harm is increasingly being viewed as a more productive mechanism through which to engage with misinformation and disinformation as a paradigm (as discussed in Section 1).

Could democratisation be taken further? A productive proposal comes from Lauren Naudts and colleagues (2025), who call for co-design initiatives as well as spaces for individuals and community groups to give feedback during a recommender system's development, and for these actors, along with experts and regulators, to assess the performance of the system after the fact, and offers space for people to actively contribute to the development of recommendation systems. The logic of the 'right to constructive optimization that promotes people's effective enjoyment of fundamental rights and civic values' that Naudts and colleagues (2025) propose might be extended further to embrace participation by individuals and communities in the design and development of systems adopted to address misinformation and disinformation. Further research will ideally assist in helping to flesh out and respond to such ideas.

Conclusion

The aim of this Element has been to intervene in a heightened public narrative that anticipates an informational crisis fuelled by the internet, especially following the widespread adoption of AI including Generative AI. In such a context, legal solutions are increasingly being looked to as ways of addressing the spread of harmful misinformation and disinformation online. While numerous laws have been introduced, the specific legal and social contexts in which they are deployed mean that these interventions can only partially ameliorate what is a global concern. In addition, we have also noted that with legal frameworks focussed on specific harms, more long-term efforts involve addressing misinformation and disinformation at the source. To this end, we have set out both the opportunities and limits associated with current technical interventions, as well as outlined what we see as necessary social solutions.

Our purpose in this conclusion is to reiterate that because legal frameworks can only do so much and private regulation through platforms is necessary but unsuited to the task of establishing a robust information ecosystem, we need to seriously consider alternative and additional responses. We have argued throughout that a productive way to approach the harms of misinformation and disinformation is through civic and societal approaches. Rather than revisit every suggestion we have made along these lines, we focus in this conclusion on three of what we view to be the most consequential steps to take right now and take the opportunity to flesh them out in more detail.

The first is establishing algorithmic systems that do not simply optimise for engagement. Much of the concerns about the spread of misinformation and disinformation have emerged because content has been spread with the goal of seeking profit rather than with a wider civic intentionality. While similar criticisms could be made about private broadcast media companies, they at least acknowledged their civic commitments, even if such commitments were usually honoured in the breach. Today, there has been significant work across media studies, law and the recommender system community attempting to establish normative baselines for these technologies, with a significant amount of work being done around diversity (Vrijenhoek et al., 2024). Other efforts borrow from journalistic practices and assess how editorial decision-making intersects with algorithmic deployment (Møller, 2022).

Observability is the second key intervention, allowing us to see what goes on within (and across) platform ecosystems. As noted earlier, the EU DSA enables research access to data, which has previously been withheld or handed out selectively to specific researchers (Bruns, 2021). However, implementation is ongoing and is largely at the pilot project stage. Various researchers have stepping into this gap to address the issue. Notable mixed-methods work has been conducted by Quya Kong and colleagues (2022), drawing on data from APIs, machine learning and detailed ethnographic work to track the spread of 'problematic speech'. Other research teams are developing citizen science methods, encouraging individuals to donate data to allow scholars to analyse the spread of information online (Meese, Albarrán-Torres, Albury et al., 2024). Given the amount of noise and debate around the topic of misinformation and disinformation, empirical clarity around the actual spread and impact of the issue is critical.

Finally, establishing literacies around media and digital technology is needed. Media literacy is a well-established intervention strategy but as we have seen, its deployment across national educational curriculums is haphazard. There is also little serious engagement with algorithmic literacy yet, which only just starting to emerge as a scholarly paradigm. Given the centrality of recommender systems and content moderation to the spread of content, understanding how these technologies work becomes increasingly critical for audiences seeking to understand misinformation and disinformation. Looking ahead, we might also try to account for industrial and economic literacies associated with the production of this sort of content. Jonathon Corpus Ong and Ross Tapsell's significant ethnographic work (2022) has revealed the formal and informal economies that undergird the spread of disinformation and the extent to which it aligns with, or is even included in, business-as-usual across the media industries, from public relations to influencer marketing.

These efforts point to the importance of not just identifying harms associated with misinformation and disinformation but also accounting for the information ecosystem in its entirety. Efforts like fact-checking and literacy initiatives (for example) can provide some assistance but they cannot substitute for a layered approach that can identify and address harms where they occur. Are individuals being targeted? Are communities losing trust in reliable media sources? Or perhaps, intermediaries are amplifying incorrect information (knowingly or unknowingly). Once the relevant issue is accounted for, we can draw on legal, social and technical remedies as needed. However, taking this pathway requires commentators and stakeholders to produce more rigorous data and approach the reform of the information ecosystem with a view towards resilience from a place of care and improvement.

Mihailidis' (2018) 'civic intentionality' offers one way forward. Moving beyond the corrective impulses of media literacy, he calls for participatory media ethic, one that creates spaces within and around the media ecosystem, where people are invited to not just consume information but to shape informational futures. Doing so allows us to recognise that people are not merely consumers of (or audiences for) either misinformation and disinformation or authoritative sources. We are citizens who should not only have a stake in our information environment, but also actively participate in it. Ensuing that this participation can take place means that a much wider programme involving trust-building and the democratisation of the media environment needs to occur before these sorts of modes of engagement can be established. Yet it is hard to build and sustain the civic practices and modes of sociality that will sufficiently address the spread of misinformation and disinformation.

The current political and policy discussion surrounding AI and misinformation and disinformation can easily prompt a sense of concern and even panic. Already, we have seen how legal solutions are being looked to as a way of addressing these along with their harms. Technical solutions are also constantly being explored. In such a context, this Element has highlighted the importance also of explicitly social dimensions, geared to balancing different perspectives and inviting participants to consider viewing information environments as living civic spaces where all of society comes to engage. They are not spaces that can just be fixed, corrected or cleansed. They need to be treated like all environments, where healthy ecosystems can only emerge from careful stewardship and tending, and a much slower process of restoration and repair. We hope our Element has offered some useful ideas on practical pathways forward.

References

Abels, G. (2022). What Is the Future of Automated Fact-Checking? Fact-Checkers Discuss. www.poynter.org/fact-checking/2022/how-will-automated-fact-checking-work/.

ACCC (Australian Competition and Consumer Commission) (2022). ACCC Takes Action over Alleged Misleading Conduct by Meta for Publishing Scam Celebrity Crypto Ads on Facebook. www.accc.gov.au/media-release/accc-takes-action-over-alleged-misleading-conduct-by-meta-for-publishing-scam-celebrity-crypto-ads-on-facebook.

Agarwal, S., Farid, H., Fried, O. and Agrawala, M. (2020). Detecting Deep-Fake Videos from Phoneme-Viseme Mismatches. *2020 IEEE/CVF Conference on Computer Vision and Pattern Recognition Workshops (CVPRW). 2020 IEEE/CVF Conference on Computer Vision and Pattern Recognition Workshops (CVPRW)*, Seattle, WA, USA: IEEE: 2814–2822. https://doi.org/10.1109/CVPRW50498.2020.00338.

AI Elections Accord (2025). *A Tech Accord to Combat Deceptive Use of AI in 2024 Elections.* www.ncsl.org/technology-and-communication/deceptive-audio-or-visual-media-deepfakes-2024-legislation.

Akers, J., Bansal, G., Cadamuro, G. et al. (2018). Technology-Enabled Disinformation: Summary, Lessons, and Recommendations. *Technical Report UW-CSE.* https://arxiv.org/abs/1812.09383.

Albert, J. (2024). TikTok and the Romanian Elections: A Stress Test for DSA Enforcement. https://dsa-observatory.eu/2024/12/20/tiktok-and-the-romanian-elections/.

Altay, S. (2022). How Effective Are Interventions against Misinformation? https://doi.org/10.31234/osf.io/sm3vk.

Altay, S., Kleis Nielsen, R. and Fletcher, R. (2022). Quantifying the 'Infodemic': People Turned to Trustworthy News Outlets During the 2020 Coronavirus Pandemic. *Journal of Quantitative Description: Digital Media*, 2. https://doi.org/10.51685/jqd.2022.020.

Altay, S., Nielsen, R. K. and Fletcher, R. (2024). News Can Help! The Impact of News Media and Digital Platforms on Awareness of and Belief in Misinformation. *The International Journal of Press/Politics*, 29(2): 459–484. https://doi.org/10.1177/19401612221148981.

Andrejevic, M. (2025). Don't Rely on Social Media Users for Fact-Checking. Many Don't Care Much about the Common Good. *The Conversation.* https://theconversation.com/dont-rely-on-social-media-users-for-fact-checking-many-dont-care-much-about-the-common-good-246977.

Are, C. (2024). The Assemblages of Flagging and De-Platforming against Marginalised Content Creators. *Convergence: The International Journal of Research into New Media Technologies*, 30(2): 922–937. https://doi.org/10.1177/13548565231218629.

Asr, F. T. and Taboada, M. (2019). Big Data and Quality Data for Fake News and Misinformation Detection. *Big Data & Society*: 1–14. https://doi.org/10.1177/2053951719843310.

Associated Press (2025). Settlement Reached in Investors' Lawsuit against Mark Zuckerberg and other Company Leaders, July 18. www.securityweek.com/settlement-reached-in-investors-lawsuit-against-meta-ceo-mark-zuckerberg-and-other-company-leaders/.

Australian Competition and Consumer Commission (2025). ACCC Welcomes Passage of World-First Scam Prevention Laws. www.accc.gov.au/media-release/accc-welcomes-passage-of-world-first-scams-prevention-laws.

Australian Consumer Law (2010). Australian Competition and Consumer Act 2010 (Cth): Schedule 2.

Australian Electoral Commission (2025). Stop and Consider … What You See, Hear and Read about the Voting Process. www.aec.gov.au/Elections/electoral-advertising/stopandconsider.htm.

Authenticity (2025). X Help Centre. https://help.x.com/en/rules-and-policies/authenticity.

Badshah, N. (2024). Children to be Taught How to Spot Extremist Content and Fake News Online. *The Guardian*, 10 August. www.theguardian.com/education/article/2024/aug/10/uk-children-to-be-taught-how-to-spot-extremist-content-and-misinformation-online.

Balkin, J. M. (2018). Free Speech in the Algorithmic Society: Big Data, Private Governance, and New School Speech Regulation. *UC Davis Law Review*, 51: 1149–1240. https://doi.org/10.2139/ssrn.3038939.

Barbrook, R. and Cameron, A. (1996). The Californian Ideology. *Science as Culture*, 6(1): 44–72. https://doi.org/10.1080/09505439609526455.

Birrer, A. and Just, N. (2024). What We Know and Don't Know about Deepfakes: An Investigation into the State of the Research and Regulatory Landscape. *New Media & Society*. https://doi.org/10.1177/14614448241253138.

Bogost, I. (2025). Fact-Checking Was Too Good for Facebook. *The Atlantic*, January 8. www.theatlantic.com/technology/archive/2025/01/facebook-end-fact-checking/681253/.

Bontridder, N. and Poullet, Y. (2021). The Role of Artificial Intelligence in Disinformation. *Data & Policy*, e32(3): 1–20. https://doi.org/10.1017/dap.2021.20.

Brasoveanu, A. M. P. and Andonie, R. (2021). Integrating Machine Learning Techniques in Semantic Fake News Detection. *Neural Processing Letters*, 53: 3055–3072. https://doi.org/10.1007/s11063-020-10365-x53.

Britton, A. (2025). The Delicate Balance: Freedom of Speech, Evidence-Based Discourse and the Challenge of Conspiracy Theories in the Digital Age. www.linkedin.com/pulse/delicate-balance-freedom-speech-evidence-based-theories-britton-uq0xe.

Bruns, A. (2021). After the 'APIcalypse': Social Media Platforms and Their Fight against Critical Scholarly Research. In S. Walker, D. Mercea and M. Bastos, eds. *Disinformation and Data Lockdown on Social Platforms*. London: Routledge: 14–36.

Bruns, A. (2023). Revisiting Key Concepts in Digital Media Research: Influence, Populism, Partisanship, Polarisation. *AoIR Selected Papers of Internet Research*. https://doi.org/10.5210/spir.v2023i0.13527.

Bruns, A., Harrington, S. and Hurcombe, E. (2021). Coronavirus Conspiracy Theories: Tracing Misinformation Trajectories from the Fringes to the Mainstream. In M. Lewis, E. Govender and K. Holland, eds., *Communicating COVID-19: Interdisciplinary Perspectives*. Switzerland: Springer: 229–249.

Burgess, J. (2023). Everyday Data Cultures: Beyond Big Critique and the Technological Sublime. *AI & SOCIETY*, 38(3): 1243–1244. https://doi.org/10.1007/s00146-022-01503-1.

Burgess, J., Carah, N., Angus, D., Obeid, A. and Andrejevic, M. (2024). Why Am I Seeing This Ad? The Affordances and Limits of Automated User-Level Explanation in Meta's Advertising System. *New Media & Society*, 26(9): 5130–5149. https://doi.org/10.1177/14614448241251796.

Burney, M. (2023). New Jersey Becomes First State to Require Media Literacy for K-12. government technology. www.govtech.com/education/k-12/new-jersey-becomes-first-state-to-require-media-literacy-for-k-12.

Cademix (2025). *The Death of Fact-Checking? How Major Platforms Are Redefining Truth in the Digital Age*. Cademix Institute of Technology. www.cademix.org/the-death-of-fact-checking-how-major-platforms-are-redefining-truth-in-the-digital-age/.

California Consumer Privacy Act (CCPA) (2018). Cal. Civ. Code § 1798.100 et seq.

California Penal Code § 647 (2024).

California Privacy Rights Act (CPRA) (2020).

California Senate Bill (SB) 243 (2025). An Act to add Chapter 22.6 (commencing with Section 22601) to Division 8 of the Business and Professions Code, relating to Artificial Intelligence.

Canaan, I. (2022). NetzDG and the German Precedent for Authoritarian Creep and Authoritarian Learning. *Columbia Journal of European Law*, 28(1): 101–133.

Caplan, S. (2024). Unregulated Online Political Ads Pose a Threat to Democracy. *The Conversation*. https://theconversation.com/unregulated-online-political-ads-pose-a-threat-to-democracy-231268.

Carah, N., Hayden, L., Brown, M.-G. et al. (2024). Observing 'Tuned' Advertising on Digital Platforms. *Internet Policy Review*, 13(2). https://doi.org/10.14763/2024.2.1779.

Chen, S. (2023). Regulating Online Hate Speech: The Singapore Experiment. *International Review of Law, Computers and Technology*: 1–21. https://doi.org/10.1080/13600869.2023.2295091.

Chesney, B. and Citron, D. (2019). Deep Fakes: A Looming Challenge for Privacy, Democracy, and National Security. *California Law Review*, 107(6): 1753–1786. http://dx.doi.org/10.2139/ssrn.3213954.

Chesterman, S. (2021). *We, the Robots?: Regulating Artificial Intelligence and the Limits of the Law*. Cambridge University Press. https://doi.org/10.1017/9781009047081.

Chesterman, S. (2025). Lawful but Awful: Evolving Legislative Responses to Address Online Misinformation, Disinformation, and Mal-Information in the Age of Generative AI, *The American Journal of Comparative Law*: 933–965, avaf020. https://doi.org/10.1093/ajcl/avaf020.

Children's Online Privacy Protection Act (COPPA) (1998). 15 US Code Chapter 91.

Chin, S. (2024). Bill to Combat Digitally Manipulated Content, Deepfakes During Elections Tabled in Parliament. *Straits Times*. www.straitstimes.com/singapore/politics/bill-passed-to-counter-digitally-manipulated-content-deepfakes-during-election.

Citizen.org (2025). Tracker: State Legislation on Deepfakes in Elections. www.citizen.org/article/tracker-legislation-on-deepfakes-in-elections/.

Citron, D. K. (2020). A New Compact for Sexual Privacy. *William & Mary Law Review*, 62(6): 1763–1840. https://ssrn.com/abstract=3633336.

Clifford, D., Goldenfein, J., Jimenez, A. and Richardson, M. (2023). A Right of Social Dialogue on Automated Decision-Making. *Technology and Regulation*: 1–9. https://doi.org/10.26116/techreg.2023.001.

Coe, P. (2021). *Media Freedom in the Age of Citizen Journalism*. Edward Elgar Publishing: 1–308.

Coe, P. (2023). Journalism Has Changed: A New Standards Code for Modern Journalism. *Inforrm's Blog*. https://inforrm.org/2023/03/01/

journalism-has-changed-a-new-standards-code-for-modern-journalism-peter-coe/.

Coe, P. (2024). Tackling Online False Information in the United Kingdom: The Online Safety Act 2023 and Its Disconnection from Free Speech Law and Theory. *Journal of Media Law*, 15(2): 213–42. https://doi.org/10.1080/17577632.2024.2316360.

Commissioner Initiated Investigation Into Clearview AI, Inc. (Privacy) (2021). AICmr54 (14 October 2021).

Commonwealth Electoral Act (1918). (Cth) (Australia).

Communications Decency Act (CDA) (1999). 47 US Code 230.

Corser, K., Dezuanni, M. and Notley, T. (2022). How News Media Literacy Is Taught in Australian Classrooms. *The Australian Educational Researcher*, 49(4): 761–777. https://doi.org/10.1007/s13384-021-00457-5.

Cotter, K., DeCook, J. R. and Kanthawala, S. (2022). Fact-Checking the Crisis: COVID-19, Infodemics, and the Platformization of Truth. *Social Media + Society*, 8(1): 20563051211069048. Available at: https://doi.org/10.1177/20563051211069048.

Countering Foreign Propaganda and Disinformation Act (CFPDA) (2016) (US).

Cram, I. (2019). Keeping the Demos out of Liberal Democracy? Participatory Politics, 'Fake News' and the Online Speaker. *Journal of Media Law*: 113–141. https://doi.org/10.1080./17577632.2019.1697477.

Crawford, K. (2016). Can an Algorithm Be Agonistic? Ten Scenes from Life in Calculated Publics. *Science, Technology & Human Values*, 41(1): 77–92. https://doi.org/10.1177/0162243915589635.

Crawford, K. and Gillespie, T. (2016). What Is a Flag For? Social Media Reporting Tools and the Vocabulary of Complaint, *New Media & Society*, 18(3): 410–428. https://doi.org/10.1177/1461444814543163.

Crime and Policing Bill (2025) (HC Bill 110, 2024–25) (UK).

Criminal Code Amendment (Deepfake Sexual Material) Act (2024) (Cth).

Criminal Code Amendment (Hate Crimes) Act (2024) (Cth) (Australia).

Croft, D. (2024). US Senate Passes Federal Bill Making Deepfake Revenge Porn Illegal. *Cyberdaily.au*. www.cyberdaily.au/security/11479-us-senate-passes-federal-bill-making-deepfake-revenge-porn-illegal.

Cyberspace Administration of China (2023). Interim Measures for the Management of Generative Artificial Intelligence Services, promulgated by the Cyberspace Administration of China, National Development and Reform Commission; Ministry of Education,

Ministry of Science and Technology, Ministry of Industry and Information Technology, Ministry of Public Security, National Radio and Television Administration. www.cac.gov.cn/2023-07/13/c_1690898327029107.htm.

Cyberspace Administration of China (2025). Notice by the Cyberspace Administration of China, the Ministry of Industry and Information Technology, the Ministry of Public Security, and the National Radio and Television Administration of Issuing the Measures for Identification of Artificial Intelligence: Generated Synthetic Contents. http://www.lawinfochina.com/display.aspx?id=44383&lib=law.

Das, A., Liu, H., Kovatchev, V. and Lease, M. (2023). The State of Human-Centered NLP Technology for Fact-Checking. *Information Processing & Management*, 60(2): 103219. https://doi.org/10.1016/j.ipm.2022.103219.

Davis, M. (2024). At Your Discretion. Centre for Media Transition, University of Technology Sydney. www.uts.edu.au/news/2024/09/your-discretion.

Davis, M. and Molitorisz, S. (2025). Promoting Rights and Accountability in the Regulation of Misinformation. *Australian Journal of Human Rights*, 30(2): 1–28. https://doi.org/10.1080/1323238X.2025.2466862.

Delcker, J. (2020). How Cambridge Analytica Used AI – No, Google Didn't Call for a Ban on Face Recognition – Restricting AI Exports. *Politico EU*. www.politico.eu/newsletter/ai-decoded/politico-ai-decoded-how-cambridge-analytica-used-ai-no-google-didnt-call-for-a-ban-on-face-recognition-restricting-ai-exports/.

DeNardis, L. and Hackl, A. M. (2015). Internet Governance *by* Social Media Platforms. *Telecommunications Policy*, 39(9): 761–770. https://doi.org/10.1016/j.telpol.2015.04.003.

Department of Infrastructure, T. (2025). Statutory Review of the Online Safety Act 2021. www.infrastructure.gov.au/have-your-say/statutory-review-online-safety-act-2021.

Dierickx, L., Lindén, C.-G., Opdahl, A. L. (2023). Automated Fact-Checking to Support Professional Practices: Systematic Literature Review and Meta-Analysis. *International Journal of Communication*, 17: 1570–1590. https://ijoc.org/index.php/ijoc/article/view/21071.

Directive 2005/29/EC of the European Parliament and of the Council. Unfair Commercial Practices Directive.

Dixit, A., Kaur, N. and Kingra, S. (2023). Review of Audio Deepfake Detection Techniques: Issues and Prospects. *Expert Systems*, 40(8): e13322. https://doi.org/10.1111/exsy.13322.

Dobber, T., Metoui, N., de Vreese, C. et al. (2021). Do (Targeted) Deepfakes Have Real Effects on Political Attitudes? *The International Journal of Press/Politics*, 26(1): 69–91. https://doi.org/10.1177/1940161220944364.

Dogruel, L. (2021). Folk Theories of Algorithmic Operations during Internet Use: A Mixed Methods Study. *The Information Society*, 37(5): 287–298. https://doi.org/10.1080/01972243.2021.1949768.

Dogruel, L., Masur, P. and Joeckel, S. (2022). Development and Validation of an Algorithm Literacy Scale for Internet Users. *Communication Methods and Measures*, 16(2): 115–133. https://doi.org/10.1080/19312458.2021.1968361.

Douek, E. (2024). The Meta Oversight Board and the Empty Promise of Legitimacy. *Harvard Journal of Law & Technology*, 37(2): 373–445. http://dx.doi.org/10.2139/ssrn.4565180.

Douek, E. (2025). The Politics and Perverse Effects of the Fight against Online Medical Misinformation. *Yale Law Journal Forum*, 134: 237–269. http://dx.doi.org/10.2139/ssrn.5207339.

Downes, L. (2009). *The Laws of Disruption: Harnessing the New Forces That Govern Life and Business in the Digital Age*. Basic Books.

Drolsbach, C., Solovev, K. and Prollochs, N. (2024). Community Notes Increase Trust in Fact-Checking on Social Media. *PNAS Nexus*, 3: 1–14. https://doi.org/10.1093/pnasnexus/pgae217.

Dufour, N. and Gully, A. (2019). Contributing Data to Deepfake Detection Research. https://research.google/blog/contributing-data-to-deepfake-detection-research/.

Duivenvoorde, B. (2025). Generative AI and the Future of Marketing: A Consumer Protection Perspective. *Computer Law and Security Review*, 57: 106141. https://doi.org/10.1016/j.clsr.2025.106141.

Durbin, D. (2025). Durbin, Graham, Reps. Ocasio-Cortex & Lee Introduce Bipartisan Legislation to Combat Non-Consensual, Sexually-Explicit Deepfake Imagery. www.durbin.senate.gov/newsroom/press-releases/durbin-graham-reps-ocasio-cortez-and-lee-introduce-bipartisan-legislation-to-combat-non-consensual-sexually-explicit-deepfake-imagery.

Ecker, U. K. H., Lewandowsky, S., Coo, J. et al. (2022). The Psychological Drivers of Misinformation Belief and Its Resistance to Correction. *Nature Reviews Psychology*, 1(1): 13–29. https://doi.org/10.1038/s44159-021-00006-y.

Ecker, U. K. H., Roozenbeek, J., van der Linden, S. et al. (2024). Misinformation Poses a Bigger Threat to Democracy than You

Might Think. *Nature*, 630(8015): 29–32. https://doi.org/10.1038/d41586-024-01587-3.

Edwards, P., Nebel, J.-C., Greenhill, D. and Liang, X. (2024). A Review of Deepfake Techniques: Architecture, Detection, and Datasets. *IEEE Access*, 12: 154718–154742. https://doi.org/10.1109/ACCESS.2024.3477257.

eSafety Commissioner (2024). Best Practice Framework for Online Safety Education. www.esafety.gov.au/educators/best-practice-framework.

eSafety Commissioner v. *Rotondo* (No 4) (2025) FCA 1191.

European Commission (2024). Questions and Answers on the Digital Services Act. https://ec.europea.eu/commission/presscorner/detail/en/qanda_20_2348.

European Commission (2025a). Supervision of the Designated Very Large Online Platforms and Search Engines under DSA. https://digital-strategy.ec.europa.eu/en/policies/list-designated-vlops-and-vloses.

European Commission (2025b). New EU Rules on Political Advertising Come into Effect. https://commission.europa.eu/news-and-media/news/new-eu-rules-political-advertising-come-effect-2025-10-10_en.

European Parliamentary Research Service (2024). Information Integrity Online and the European Democracy Shield. www.europarl.europa.eu/RegData/etudes/BRIE/2024/767153/EPRS_BRI(2024)767153_EN.pdf.

European Union (2000). Charter of Fundamental Rights of the European Union, 7 December 2000, OJ C364/1.

Farkas, J. and Schou, J. (2019). *Post-Truth, Fake News and Democracy: Mapping the Politics of Falsehood.* Routledge.

Federal Communications Commission (2024a). FCC Fines Man Behind Election Interference Scheme $6 Million for Sending Illegal Robocalls That Used Deepfake Generative AI Technology. https://docs.fcc.gov/public/attachments/DOC-405811A1.pdf.

Federal Communications Commission (2024b). In the Matter of Disclosure and Transparency of Artificial Intelligence-Generated Content in Political Advertisements. https://docs.fcc.gov/public/attachments/FCC-24-74A1.pdf.

Federal Trade Commission (2019a). FTC Imposes $5 Billion Penalty and Sweeping New Privacy Restrictions on Facebook. www.ftc.gov/news-events/news/press-releases/2019/07/ftc-imposes-5-billion-penalty-sweeping-new-privacy-restrictions-facebook.

Federal Trade Commission (2019b). FTC Issues Opinion and Order against Cambridge Analytica for Deceiving Consumers about the Collection of Facebook Data, Compliance with EU-U.S. Privacy Shield.

Federal Trade Commission (2024). FTC Announces Crackdown on Deceptive AI Claims and Schemes. www.ftc.gov/news-events/news/press-releases/2024/09/ftc-announces-crackdown-deceptive-ai-claims-schemes.

Ferrucci, P. (2019). The End of Ombudsmen? 21st-Century Journalism and Reader Representatives. *Journalism & Mass Communication Quarterly*, 96(1): 288–307. https://doi.org/10.1177/1077699018805986.

Fischman-Afori, O. (2023). Regulating Online Content Moderation: Taking Stock and Moving Ahead with Procedural Justice and Due Process Rights. In J. Schovsbo, ed., *The Exploitation of Intellectual Property Rights: In Search of the Right Balance*. Cheltenham: Edward Elgar: 5–27.

Flam, F. (2024). Commentary: Elon Musk's Community Notes Feature on X Is Working. *The Conversation*. https://theconversation.com/dont-rely-on-social-media-users-for-fact-checking-many-dont-care-much-about-the-common-good-246977.

Flew, T. (2021). *Regulating Platforms*. Cambridge: Polity Press.

Flew, T. (2024). Mediated Trust, the Internet and Artificial Intelligence: Ideas, Interests, Institutions and Futures. *Policy & Internet*, 16(2): 443–457. https://doi.org/10.1002/poi3.390.

Flew, T., Suzor, N. and Martin, F. (2019). Internet Regulation as Media Policy: Rethinking the Question of Digital Communication Platform Governance. *International Journal of Digital Television*, 10(1): 33–50. https://doi.org/10.1386/jdtv.10.1.33_1.

Foreign Influence Transparency Scheme Act (2018) (Cth) (Australia).

Foreign Interference (Countermeasures) Act (2021) (Singapore).

Forrest v. *Meta Platforms, Inc.* (2024) 737 F Supp 3d 808 (N. D. Cal., 17 June).

Fragale, M. and Grilli, V. (2024). Deepfake, Deep Trouble: The European AI Act and the Fight against AI-Generated Misinformation. *Columbia Journal of European Law*. https://cjel.law.columbia.edu/preliminary-reference/2024/deepfake-deep-trouble-the-european-ai-act-and-the-fight-against-ai-generated-misinformation/.

Gerbrandt, R.-L. (2023). Threatening and Protecting Press Publishers and Journalism in the UK's Regulation of Social Media Platforms. *Journal of Media Law*: 1–35. https://doi.org/10.1080/17577632.2024.2445897.

Gilbert, S. (2025). Three Reasons Meta Will Struggle with Community Fact-Checking. www.technologyreview.com/2025/01/29/1110630/three-reasons-meta-will-struggle-with-community-fact-checking/.

Gillespie, T. (2018a). *Custodians of the Internet: Platforms, Content Moderation, and the Hidden Decisions that Shape Social Media*. Yale University Press.

Gillespie, T. (2018b). Platforms Are Not Intermediaries. *Georgetown Law Technology Review*, 2(2): 198–216. https://georgetownlawtechreview.org/wp-content/uploads/2018/07/2.2-Gilespie-pp-198-216.pdf.

Gillespie, T. (2020). Content Moderation, AI, and the Question of Scale. *Big Data & Society*, 7(2): 2053951720943234. https://doi.org/10.1177/2053951720943234.

Gillespie, T. (2022). Do Not Recommend? Reduction as a Form of Content Moderation. *Social Media + Society*, 8(3): 20563051221117552. https://doi.org/10.1177/20563051221117552.

Gillespie, T., Aufderheide, P., Carmi, E. et al. (2020). Expanding the Debate about Content Moderation: Scholarly Research Agendas for the Coming Policy Debates. *Internet Policy Review*, 9(4). https://policyreview.info/articles/analysis/expanding-debate-about-content-moderation-scholarly-research-agendas-coming-policy.

Ginsburg, J. C. and Austin, G. W. (2025). Deepfakes in Domestic and International Perspective. *Columbia Journal of Law & the Arts*, 48(3): 297–324. https://scholarship.law.columbia.edu/faculty_scholarship/4640.

Glas, R., van Vught, J., Fluitsma, T. et al. (2023). Literacy at Play: An Analysis of Media Literacy Games Used to Foster Media Literacy Competencies. *Frontiers in Communication*, 8. https://doi.org/10.3389/fcomm.2023.1155840.

Goodman, M. (2023). Does the First Amendment Protect Free Speech or Threats and Scams? *Media Watch*, 14(3) 403–439. 3. https://doi.org/10.1177/09760911231179002.

Gorwa, R., Binns, R. and Katzenbach, C. (2020). Algorithmic Content Moderation: Technical and Political Challenges in the Automation of Platform Governance. *Big Data & Society*, 7(1). 205395171989794. https://doi.org/10.1177/2053951719897945.

Grantham, S. (2025). The AEC Wants to Stop AI and Misinformation. But It's Up against a Problem That Is Deep and Dark. *The Conversation*. https://theconversation.com/the-aec-wants-to-stop-ai-and-misinformation-but-its-up-against-a-problem-that-is-deep-and-dark-248773.

Graves, L. (2018). Boundaries Not Drawn: Mapping the Institutional Roots of the Global Fact-Checking Movement. *Journalism Studies*, 19(5): 613–631. https://doi.org/10.1080/1461670X.2016.1196602.

Guo, Z., Schlichtkrull, M. and Vlachos, A. (2022). A Survey on Automated Fact-Checking. *Transactions of the Association for Computational Linguistics*, 10: 178–206. https://doi.org/10.1162/tacl_a_00454.

Habgood-Coote, J. (2023). Deepfakes and the Epistemic Apocalypse. *Synthese*, 201(3): 103. https://doi.org/10.1007/s11229-023-04097-3.

Hao, K. (2021). Deepfake Porn Is Ruining Women's Lives. Now the Law May Finally Ban It. MIT Technology Review. www.technologyreview.com/2021/02/12/1018222/deepfake-revenge-porn-coming-ban/.

Harding, L., Paterson, J. and Bant, E. (2022). ACCC vs Big Tech: Round 10 and Counting. *Pursuit*, 24 March. https://pursuit.unimelb.edu.au/articles/accc-vs-big-tech-round-10-and-counting.

Harrison, K. and Leopold, A. (2021). How Blockchain Can Help Combat Disinformation. *HBR*. https://hbr.org/2021/07/how-blockchain-can-help-combat-disinformation.

Helberger, N. and Vreese, C. (2024). Caught between Grand Ambitions and Small Print: The AI Act and the Use of Gen AI in Elections. *Internet Policy Review*. www.ncsl.org/technology-and-communication/deceptive-audio-or-visual-media-deepfakes-2024-legislation.

Husovec, M. (2024a). The Digital Services Act's Red Line: What the Commission Can and Cannot Do about Disinformation. *Journal of Media Law*, 16(1): 47–56. https://doi.org/10.1080/17577632.2024.2362483.

Husovec, M. (2024b). *Principles of the Digital Services Act*. Oxford University Press. https://doi.org/10.1093/law-ocl/9780192882455.003.0021.

IDEA (2024). *The 2024 Global Elections Super-Cycle*. www.idea.int/initiatives/the-2024-global-elections-supercycle.

Info-Communications Media Development Authority (IMDA) (2025). Enhancing Online Safety in Singapore. www.imda.gov.sg/regulations-and-licensing-listing/content-standards-and-classification/standards-and-classification/internet/online-safety.

In Re Clearview AI Consumer Privacy Litigation (2025). Public Citizen. www.citizen.org/litigation/in-re-clearview-ai-consumer-privacy-litigation/.

In Re Facebook, Inc. Consumer Privacy User Profile Litigation (2018). No. 3:18-md-02843, 655 F. Supp. 3d 899 (N. D. Cal. 2018).

Jacobs, L. G. (2022). Freedom of Speech and Regulation of Fake News. *The American Journal of Comparative Law*, 70: 278–311.: https://doi.org/10.1093/ajcl/avac010.

Jahangir, R. (2025a). EU Steps Up Civil Society Engagement on the Digital Services Act – Is It Enough? www.techpolicy.press/-eu-steps-up-civil-society-engagement-on-the-digital-services-act-is-it-enough/.

Jahangir, R. (2025b). Understanding the EU's Digital Services Act Enforcement against X. www.techpolicy.press/understanding-the-eus-digital-services-act-enforcement-against-x/.

Jungherr, A. (2024). Foundational Questions for the Regulation of Digital Disinformation. *Journal of Media Law*, 16(1): 8–17. https://doi.org/10.1080/17577632.2024.2362484.

Kalla, J. L. and Broockman, D. E. (2018). The Minimal Persuasive Effects of Campaign Contact in General Elections: Evidence from 49 Field Experiments. *American Political Science Review*, 112(1): 148–166. https://doi.org/10.1017/S0003055417000363.

Kalpokas, I. (2021). Problematising Reality: The Promises and Perils of Synthetic Media. *SN Social Sciences*, 1(1): 1–11. https://doi .org/10.1007/s43545-020-00010-8.

Katsirea, I. (2018). 'Fake News': Reconsidering the Value of Untruthful Expression in the Face of Regulatory Uncertainty. *Journal of Media Law*, 10: 159–188.

Katsirea, I. (2024). *Press Freedom and Regulation in a Digital Era*. Oxford University Press.

Kaur, A., Noori Hoshyar, A., Saikrishna, V. et al. (2024). Deepfake Video Detection: Challenges and Opportunities. *Artificial Intelligence Review*, 57(6): 159. https://doi.org/10.1007/s10462-024-10810-6.

Kenyon, A. (2021). *Democracy of Expression: Positive Free Speech and Law*. Cambridge University Press.

Kenyon, A. (2024). Democratic Freedom of Expression and Disinformation. In Krotoszynski, R., Koltay, A. and Garden, C. eds., *Disinformation, Misinformation and Democracy*. Cambridge University Press: 50–77.

van de Kerkhof, J. (2025). Article 22 Digital Services Act: Building Trust with Trusted Flaggers. *Internet Policy Review*, 14(1). https://doi .org/10.14763/2025.1.1828.

Kertysova, K. (2018). Artificial Intelligence and Disinformation: How AI changes the Way Disinformation is Produced, Disseminated, and Can Be Countered. Security and Human Rights, 29: 55–81. https// doi.org:10.1163/18750230-02901005.

Klonick, K. (2017). The New Governors: The People, Rules and Processes Governing Online Speech, *Harvard Law Review*, 131: 1598–1670. https://ssrn.com/abstract=2937985.

Klonick, K. (2020). The Facebook Oversight Board: Creating an Independent Institution to Adjudicate Online Free Expression. *Yale Law Journal*, 129(8): 2418–2499. https://ssrn.com/abstract=3639234.

Koltay. A. (2024). Freedom of Expression and the Regulation of Disinformation in the European Union. In Krotoszynski, R., Koltay, A. and Garden, C., eds., *Disinformation, Misinformation and Democracy*. Cambridge University Press: 133–160.

Kong, Q., Booth, E., Bailo, F. et al. (2022). Slipping to the Extreme: A Mixed Method to Explain How Extreme Opinions Infiltrate Online

Discussions. *Proceedings of the International AAAI Conference on Web and Social Media*, 16: 524–535. https://doi.org/10.1609/icwsm.v16i1.19312.

Kreps, S. and Kriner, D. (2023). How AI Threatens Democracy. *Journal of Democracy*, 34(4): 122–131. https://doi.org/10.1353/jod.2023.a907693.

Lamo, M. and Calo, R. (2019). Regulating Bot Speech. *UCLA Law Review*, 66: 988–1020. http://dx.doi.org/10.2139/ssrn.3214572.

Leetaru, K. (2018). Should Social Media Be Allowed to Profit from Terrorism and Hate Speech? *Forbes*. www.forbes.com/sites/kalevleetaru/2018/12/14/should-social-media-be-allowed-to-profit-from-terrorism-and-hate-speech/.

Lessig, L. (1999). *Code and Other Laws of Cyberspace*. Basic Books.

Lessig, L. (2006). *Code Version 2.0*. Basic Books. https://lessig.org/product/codev2.

Lim, G. and Bradshaw, S. (2023). Chilling Legislation: Tracking the Impact of 'Fake News' Laws on Press Freedom Internationally. Centre for International Media Assistance. www.cima.ned.org/publication/chilling-legislation/.

Livingstone, S. (2015). Active Audiences? The Debate Progresses But Is Far from Resolved: *Communication Theory*, 25(4): 439–446. https://doi.org/10.1111/comt.12078.

Lorenz-Spreen, P., Oswald, L., Lewandowsky, S. and Hertwig, R. (2022). A Systematic Review of Worldwide Causal and Correlational Evidence on Digital Media and Democracy. *Nature Human Behaviour*, 7(1): 74–101. https://doi.org/10.1038/s41562-022-01460-1.

Main, N. (2022). TikTok Wants to Be More Transparent with Its Algorithm. *Gizmodo*. https://gizmodo.com/tiktok-algorithm-why-this-video-social-media-1849914262.

Manning, C. (2022). Human Language Understanding & Reasoning. *Daedalus*, 151(2): 127–138. https://doi.org/10.1162/daed_a_01905.

Marchal, N., Xu, R., Elasmar, R. et al. (2024). Generative AI Misuse: A Taxonomy of Tactics and Insights from Real-World Data. arXiv. https://doi.org/10.48550/arXiv.2406.13843.

Marques, M. D., Ling, M., Williams, M. N. et al. (2022). Australasian Public Awareness and Belief in Conspiracy Theories: Motivational Correlates. *Political Psychology*, 43(1): 177–198. https://doi.org/10.1111/pops.12746.

Marsden, C. T. and Meyer, T. (2019). Regulating disinformation with artificial intelligence: effects of disinformation initiatives on freedom of expression and media pluralism. Panel for the Future of Science and Technology European Science-Media Hub. European Parliamentary Research Service. https://doi.org/10.2861/003689.

Marsoof, A., Luco, A., Tan, H. and Joty, S. (2023). Content-Filtering AI Systems – Limitations, Challenges and Regulatory Approaches. *Information and Communications Technology Law*, 32(1): 64–101. https://doi.org/10.1080/13600834.2022.2078395.

Mazurczyk, W., Lee, D. and Vlachos, A. (2023). Disinformation 2.0 in the Age of AI: A Cybersecurity Perspective. *Computers and Society*, 1(1): 1–5 https://doi.org/10.48550/arXiv.2306.05569.

Meese, J. and Bannerman, S. (eds) (2022). *The Algorithmic Distribution of News: Policy Responses*. Cham: Palgrave Macmillan.

Meese, J. and Hurcombe, E. (2020) *Regulating Misinformation*. Australian Policy Online: Briefing Paper, Melbourne: RMIT.

Meese, J., Albarrán-Torres, C., Albury, K. et al. (2024). ADM+S Submission to the Joint Select Committee on Social Media and Australian Society. https://apo.org.au/sites/default/files/resource-files/2024-06/apo-nid327649_0.pdf.

Meese, J., Obeid, A. K., Angus, D. and Bruns, A. (2024). Examining Exposure Diversity on Google News in Australia. *Journal of Quantitative Description: Digital Media*, 4: 1–37. https://doi.org/10.51685/jqd.2024.019.

Meta (2020). Deepfake Detection Challenge Dataset, https://ai.meta.com/datasets/dfdc/.

Meta (2025). Fact-Checked Misinformation, Transparency Centre. https://transparency.meta.com/en-gb/features/approach-to-ranking/content-distribution-guidelines/misinformation/.

Midler v. *Ford Motor Co*. 849 F.2d 460 (9th Cir. 1988).

Mihailidis, P. (2018). Civic Media Literacies: Re-Imagining Engagement for Civic Intentionality. *Learning, Media and Technology*, 43(2): 152–164. https://doi.org/10.1080/17439884.2018.1428623.

Milli, S., Carroll, M., Wang, Y. et al. (2025). Engagement Satisfaction, and the Amplification of Divisive Content on Social Media. *PNAS Nexus*, 4(3): 1–10. https://doi.org/10.1093/pnasnexus/pgaf062.

Ministry of Digital Development and Information (Singapore) (2024). MCI's Response to PQ on Regulations to Tackle Deepfake Software Used in Scam and Fraud Cases. www.mddi.gov.sg/media-centre/parliamentary-questions/pq-on-regulations-to-tackle-deepfake-software/.

Møller, L. A. (2022). Recommended for You: How Newspapers Normalise Algorithmic News Recommendation to Fit Their Gatekeeping Role. *Journalism Studies*, 23(7): 800–817. https://doi.org/10.1080/1461670X.2022.2034522.

Morrow, G., Swire-Thompson, B., Montgomery Polny, J. et al. (2022). The Emerging Science of Content Labeling: Contextualizing Social Media Content Moderation. *Journal of the Association for Information Science and Technology*, 73(10): 1365–1386. https://doi.org/10.1002/asi.24637.

National Conference of State Legislatures (NCSL) (2024). Deceptive Audio or Visual Media ('Deepfakes') 2024 Legislation. www.ncsl.org/technology-and-communication/deceptive-audio-or-visual-media-deepfakes-2024-legislation.

National Security Act (2023) (c. 32) (UK).

Naudts, L., Helberger, N., Veale, M. and Sax, M. (2025). A Right to Constructive Optimization: A Public Interest Approach to Recommender Systems in the Digital Services Act. *Journal of Consumer Policy*. https://doi.org/10.1007/s10603-025-09586-1.

Nenadić, I. (2019). Unpacking the 'European Approach' to Tackling Challenges of Disinformation and Political Manipulation. *Internet Policy Review*, 8(4). https://doi.org/10.14763/2019.4.1436.

Network Enforcement Act (NetzDG) (2017) (Germany).

Newman, N., Fletcher, R., Robertson, C. T. et al. (2024). *Reuters Institute Digital News Report 2024*. https://reutersinstitute.politics.ox.ac.uk/sites/default/files/2024-06/RISJ_DNR_2024_Digital_v10%20lr.pdf.

None Of Your Business (NYOB) (2025a). *NYOB – European Center for Digital Rights* v *OpenAI OpCo, LLC*, Case-No: C096. https://noyb.eu/sites/default/files/2025-03/OpenAI_complaint_redacted.pdf.

None Of Your Business (NOYB) (2025b). *AI Hallucinations: ChatGPT Created a Fake Child Murderer*. https://noyb.eu/en/ai-hallucinations-chatgpt-created-fake-child-murderer.

Notley, T. Chambers, S., Park, S. and Dezuanni, M. (2024). Adult Media Literacy in 2024: Australian Attitudes, Experiences and Needs. Report. Western Sydney University, Queensland University of Technology, University of Canberra. https://apo.org.au/node/327239.

Nurture Originals, Foster Art, and Keep Entertainment Safe Act (NO FAKES Act) (2025). H.R No. 2794, 119th Cong. (2025) (introduced 9 April 2025).

Nyariki, E. (2025). Fact-Checkers Are among the Top Sources for X's Community Notes, Study Reveals. www.poynter.org/ifcn/2025/fact-checkers-contribute-improve-community-notes-x/.

Nyhan, B. (2020). Facts and Myths about Misperceptions – American Economic Association. *Journal of Economic Perspectives*, 34(3), 220–236. https://doi.org/10.1257/jep.34.3.220.

Nyhan, B. and Reifler, J. (2010). When Corrections Fail: The Persistence of Political Misperceptions. *Political Behavior*, 32(2), 303–330. https://doi.org/10.1007/s11109-010-9112-2.

O'Carroll, L. and Hern, A. (2024). *EU Calls on Tech Firms to Outline Plans to Tackle Deepfakes Amid Election Fears*. www.theguardian.com/business/2024/mar/14/eu-calls-on-tech-firms-outline-plans-to-tackle-deepfakes-amid-election-fears-google-facebook-x.

OECD (2021). *The Impact of Artificial Intelligence on the Labour Market: What Do We Know So Far?* OECD Social, Employment and Migration Working Papers 256. https://doi.org/10.1787/7c895724-en.

OECD (2024). *Fakes Not Facts: Tackling Disinformationm Strengthening Information Integrity*. OECD Directorate for Public Governance. https://doi.org/10.1787/d909ff7a-en.

Oeldorf-Hirsch, A. and Neubaum, G. (2025). What Do We Know about Algorithmic Literacy? The Status Quo and a Research Agenda for a Growing field. *New Media & Society*, 27(2): 681–701. https://doi.org/10.1177/14614448231182662.

OFCOM (2023). Adults' Media Use and Attitudes Report 2023. https://www.ofcom.org.uk/siteassets/resources/documents/research-and-data/media-literacy-research/adults/adults-media-use-and-attitudes-2023/adults-media-use-and-attitudes-report-2023.pdf?v=329409

Ong, J. C. and Tapsell, R. (2022). Demystifying Disinformation Shadow Economies: Fake News Work Models in Indonesia and the Philippines. *Asian Journal of Communication*, 32(3): 251–267. https://doi.org/10.1080/01292986.2021.1971270.

Online Criminal Harms Act (2023) (Singapore).

Online Safety Act (2021) (Cth) (Australia).

Online Safety Act (2023) (c. 50) (UK).

Online Safety Amendment (Digital Duty of Care) Bill (2024) (Cth) (Australia).

Online Safety Amendment (Social Media Minimum Age) Act (2024) (Australia).

Online Safety (Miscellaneous Amendments) Act (2022) (No. 38 of 2022). Singapore.

Ortutay, B. (2025). *President Trump Signs Take It Down Act, Addressing Nonconsensual Deepfakes. What Is It?* https://thehill.com/homenews/ap/ap-business/ap-president-trump-signs-take-it-down-act-addressing-nonconsensual-deepfakes-what-is-it-2/.

Padilla, S. (2025). First-in-the-Nation AI Chatbot Safeguards Signed into Law. Press Release, 13 October. https://sd18.senate.ca.gov/news/first-nation-ai-chatbot-safeguards-signed-law.

Paris, B. and Donovan, J. (2019). Deep Fakes and Cheap Fakes: The Manipulation of Audio and Visual Evidence. Data & Society, Report. https://datasociety.net/library/deepfakes-and-cheap-fakes/.

Pasquale, F. (2025a). *Data Access and AI Explainability*. Cambridge University Press.

Pasquale, F. (2025b). AI and Electoral Manipulation: From Misinformation to Demoralization. In Diurni, A. ed., *Human Vulnerability in Interaction with AI in European Private Law*. Springer (forthcoming). https://papers.ssrn.com/sol3/papers.cfm?abstract_id=5159402.

Patel, Y., Tanwar, S., Gupta, R. and Bhattacharya, P. (2023). Deepfake Generation and Detection: Case Study and Challenges. *IEEE Access*, 11: 143296–143323. https://doi.org/10.1109/ACCESS.2023.3342107.

Paul, K. (2024). Meta overhauls rules on deepfakes, other altered media. *Reuters*. www.reuters.com/technology/cybersecurity/meta-overhauls-rules-deepfakes-other-altered-media-2024-04-05/.

Peters, J. (2023). Twitter Will Label 'Hateful' Tweets When It Restricts Them. *The Verge*. www.theverge.com/2023/4/17/23686661/twitter-label-hateful-tweets-restricts-shadowban.

Philip, H. (2020). *Lie Machines: How to Save Democracy from Troll Armies, Deceitful Robots, June News Operations, and Political Operatives*. New Haven: Yale University Press.

Pranaityte, L., Miller, J., Mesquita, L. and Murphy, S. (2024). Enhancing Media Literacy Education in Europe: Insights from the Third TeaMLit Project Report. https://media-and-learning.eu/subject/media-literacy/enhancing-media-literacy-education-in-europe-insights-from-the-third-teamlit-project-report/.

Privacy Act (1988) (Cth) (Australia).

Protection from Online Falsehoods and Manipulation Act (POFMA) (2019) (Singapore).

Protection from Scams Act (2025) (Singapore).

Public Order Act (1986) (c. 64) (UK).

PWC and Tiang & Partners (2023). Regulatory and Legislation: China's Interim Measures for the Management of Generative Artificial Intelligence Services Officially Implemented. www.pwccn.com/en/tmt/interim-measures-for-generative-ai-services-implemented-aug2023.pdf.

Racial and Religious Hatred Act (2006) (c. 1) (UK).

Radu, R. (2020). Fighting the 'Infodemic': Legal Responses to COVID-19 Disinformation. *Social Media + Society*, 6(3): 2056305120948190. https://doi.org/10.1177/2056305120948190.

Radu, R. (2025). Expert Comment: Which Urgent Tech Lessons Must the EU Take from Romania's Election? University of Oxford: News and Events. www.ox.ac.uk/news/2025-05-22-expert-comment-which-urgent-tech-lessons-must-eu-take-romania-s-election.

Rankin, J. (2025). EU Could Water Down AI Act Amid Pressure from Trump and Big Tech. *The Guardian*, 8 November. www.theguardian.com/world/2025/nov/07/european-commission-ai-artificial-intelligence-act-trump-administration-tech-business.

Regulation (EU) 2016/679 of the European Parliament and of the Council of 27 April 2016 on the Protection of Natural Persons with Regard to the Processing of Personal Data and on the Free Movement of Such Data, and Repealing Directive 95/46/EC (General Data Protection Regulation: GDPR), OJ L 119, 4 May 2016.

Regulation (EU) 2022/2065 of the European Parliament and of the Council of 19 October 2022 on a Single Market for Digital Services and Amending Directive 2000/31/EC (Digital Services Act: DSA), OJ L 277, 27 October 2022.

Regulation (EU) 2024/1689 of the European Parliament and of the Council of 13 June 2024 laying down harmonised rules on artificial intelligence and amending Regulations (Artificial Intelligence Act: AI Act), OJ L 1689, 12 July 2024.

Regulation (EU) 2024/900 on the Transparency and Targeting of Political Advertising of the European Parliament and of the Council of 13 March 2024, OJL 199, 20 March 2024.

Richmond, C. (2024). Snopes Launches FactBot, an AI Service to Fact-Check Your Questions. Snopes. www.snopes.com/2024/07/10/snopes-launches-factbot-ai-fact-checking/.

Richter, A. (2019). Disinformation in the Media under Russian Law. *IRIS Extra*, European Audiovisual Observatory, Strasbourg. https://rm.coe.int/disinformation-in-the-media-under-russian-law/1680967369.

Rieder, B. and Hofmann, J. (2020). Towards Platform Observability. *Internet Policy Review: Journal on Internet Regulation*, 9(4): 1–28. https://doi.org/10.14763/2020.4.1535.

Riley, D. (2022). Intel FakeCatcher Detects Deepfakes with a 96% Accuracy Rate. SiliconANGLE. https://siliconangle.com/2022/11/17/intel-fakecatcher-detects-deepfakes-96-accuracy-rate/.

Roberts, J., Morris, S. and Sorial, S. (2025). Combatting Mis and Disinformation in the Digital Age: Challenges and Opportunities for

Australia. *Griffith Law Review*, 34(1): 47–77. https://doi.org/10.1080/10383441.2025.2522564.

Roberts, S. T. (2019). *Behind the Screen: Content Moderation in the Shadows of Social Media*. New Haven: Yale University Press.

Robins-Early, N. (2024). ChatGPT Suspends Scarlett Johansson-Like Voice as Actor Speaks Out against OpenAI. The Guardian, 21 May. www.theguardian.com/technology/article/2024/may/20/chatgpt-scarlett-johansson-voice.

Rumyantsev, A. (2017). Russia: Information Security Doctrine, Stricter Regulations against 'Fake News' and Blocking LinkedIn. *Computer Law Review International*, 18(1): 28–32. https://doi.org/10.9785/cri-2017-0108.

Santos, Fatima and Carrilho, C. (2023). Artificial Intelligence in Automated Detection of Disinformation: A Thematic Analysis. *Journalism and Media*, 4: 679–687. https://doi.org/10.3390/journalmedia4020043.

Scams Prevention Framework Act (2025) (Cth). (Australia).

Shanmugam, K. (Minister for Home Affairs and Minister for Law). (2024). Written Reply to Parliamentary Question on Whether Protective Measures against Perpetrators Adopting Deepfake Images or Videos to Commit Offences Are Sufficient, 8 May. www.mha.gov.sg/mediaroom/parliamentary/written-reply-to-pq-on-whether-protective-measures-against-perpetrators-adopting-deepfake-images-or-videos-to-commit-offences-are-sufficient/.

Shapero, J. and Nazzaro, M. (2025). Ocasio-Cortez Renews Push against Explicit AI Deepfakes. The Hill. https://thehill.com/newsletters/technology/5312729-ocasio-cortez-renews-push-against-explicit-ai-deepfakes/.

Soon, C. and Quek, S. (2024). Safeguarding Elections from Threats Posed by Artificial Intelligence. IPS Working Papers No. 56: 1–56. https://lkyspp.nus.edu.sg/docs/default-source/ips/ips-working-paper-no-56_safeguarding-elections-from-threats-posed-by-artificial-intelligence.pdf.

Soon, C. and Tan, B. (2023). Regulating AI: Maximising Benefits and Minimising Harms, IPS Working Papers No. 52. https://lkyspp.nus.edu.sg/docs/default-source/ips/ips-working-paper-no-52_regulating-artificial-intelligence-maximising-benefits-and-minimising-harms.pdf.

Spoto, M. (2025). Musk-Challenged California Anti-Deepfake Law Struck by Judge. Bloomberg Law, 7 August. https://news.bloomberglaw.com/litigation/musk-challenged-california-anti-deepfake-law-struck-by-judge.

Starbuck v. *Meta Platforms, Inc.* (2025). CA. No. N25C-04-283, Delaware Superior Court, 29 April 2025.

Stockemer, D. and Bordeleau, J.-N. (2024). Conspiracy Theories and Their Believers in an Era of Misinformation. *Harvard Kennedy School Misinformation Review*, 5(6) https://misinforeview.hks.harvard.edu/article/conspiracy-.

Stroebel, L., Llewellyn, M., Hartley, T. et al. (2023). A Systematic Literature Review on the Effectiveness of Deepfake Detection Techniques. *Journal of Cyber Security Technology*, 7(2): 83–113. https://doi.org/10.1080/23742917.2023.2192888.

Suzor, N., Seignior, B. and Singleton, J. (2017). Non-Consensual Porn and the Responsibilities of Online Intermediaries. *Melbourne University Law Review*, 40(3): 1057–1097. https://law.unimelb.edu.au/__data/assets/pdf_file/0007/2494294/09-Suzor,-Seignior-and-Singleton.pdf.

Tan, C. (2018). *Regulating Content on Social Media: Copyright, Terms of Service and Technological Features*. London: UCL Press.

Tan, C. (2022a). Regulating Disinformation on Twitter and Facebook. *Griffith Law Review*, 31(4): 513–536. https://doi.org/10.1080/10383441.2022.2138140.

Tan, C. (2022b). The Curious Case of Regulating False News on Google. *Computer Law & Security Review*, 46: 105738. https://doi.org/10.1016/j.clsr.2022.105738.

Tan, D. and Teng, J. (2020). Fake News, Free Speech and Finding Constitutional Congruence, *Singapore Academy of Law Journal*, 32: 207–248.

TandocJr., E., Lim, Z. and Ling, R. (2018). Defining 'Fake News'. *Digital Journalism*, 6(2): 137–153. https://doi.org/10.1080/21670811.2017.1360143.

Tang, Y. (2025). MHA COS 2025: Working Together to Fight Scams. www.mha.gov.sg/home-team-news/story/detail/mha-cos-2025--working-together-to-fight-scams/.

Telephone Consumer Protection Act (TCPA) (1991). 47 USC § 227.

Teo, K. (2021). Civil Society Responses to Singapore's Online 'Fake News' Law. *International Journal of Communication*, 15: 4795–4815. https://ijoc.org/index.php/ijoc/article/view/17910.

Tkacz, N. (2014). *Wikipedia and the Politics of Openness*. Chicago, Ill: University of Chicago Press.

Tools to Address Known Exploitation by Immobilizing Technological Deepfakes on Websites and Networks (TAKE IT DOWN) Act (2025). S. 146, 119th Cong. (2025) Pub. L. No. 119-12 (US).

TU and RE v. *Google LLC* (2022). EUECJ C-460/20.

UK General Data Protection Regulation (2016). Data Protection Act 2018 c 12.

United Nations 1966, International Covenant on Civil and Political Rights, adopted 16 December 1966, entered into force 23 March 1976.

US Judiciary Committee Staff Report (2025). The Foreign Censorship Threat: How the European Union's Digital Services Act Compels Global Censorship and Infringes on American Free Speech. https://judiciary.house.gov/sites/evo-subsites/republicans-judiciary.house.gov/files/2025-07/DSA_Report%26Appendix%2807.25.25%29.pdf.

Uscinski, J., Littrell, S. and Klofstad, C. (2024). The Importance of Epistemology for the Study of Misinformation. *Current Opinion in Psychology*, 57: 101789. https://doi.org/10.1016/j.copsyc.2024.101789.

Vese, D. (2022). Governing Fake News: The Regulation of Social Media and the Right to Freedom of Expression in the Era of Emergency. *European Journal of Risk Regulation*, 13: 477–513. Available at: https://doi.org/10.1017/err.2021.48.

Video Privacy Protection Act (VIPPA) (1988). 18 USC § 2710.

Villi, M., Aharonib, T., Tenenboim-Weinblatt, K. et al. (2022). Taking a Break from News: A Five-Nation Study of News Avoidance in the Digital Era. *Digital Journalism*, 10(1): 148–164. https://doi.org/10.1080/21670811.2021.1904266.

Vinhas, O. and Bastos, M. (2023). The WEIRD Governance of Fact-Checking and the Politics of Content Moderation. *New Media & Society*, 27(5): 2768–2787. https://doi.org/10.1177/14614448231213942.

Volokh, E. (2025a). AI Libel Suit by Conservative Activist Robby Starbuck against Meta Settles. *The Volokh Conspiracy*. https://reason.com/volokh/2025/08/08/ai-libel-suit-by-conservative-activist-robby-starbuck-against-meta-settles/.

Volokh, E. (2025b). Conservative Activist Robby Starbuk Alleges Massive Defamation by Google AI. *The Volokh Conspiracy*. https://reason.com/volokh/2025/10/22/conservative-activist-robby-starbuck-alleges-massive-defamation-by-google-ai/.

Vrijenhoek, S., Daniil, S., Sandel, J. and Hollink, L. (2024). Diversity of What? On the Different Conceptualizations of Diversity in Recommender Systems. In *The 2024 ACM Conference on Fairness, Accountability, and Transparency. FAccT'24: The 2024 ACM Conference on Fairness, Accountability, and Transparency*, Rio de Janeiro Brazil: ACM: 573–584. https://doi.org/10.1145/3630106.3658926.

Watt, N., Montaña-Niño, S. and Riedlinger, M. (2025). The Art of the (Platform) Deal: Tech Platforms, Fact Checkers, and the Politics of Truth. *Weizenbaum Journal of the Digital Society*, 5(2). https://doi.org/10.34669/wi.wjds/5.2.1.

White & Case (2025). AI Watch: Global Regulatory Tracker – China. www.whitecase.com/insight-our-thinking/ai-watch-global-regulatory-tracker-china.

Wihbey, J. B. (2025a). America Must Regulate Social Media. *Time*. 20 October. https://time.com/7326940/america-must-regulate-social-media/.

Wihbey, J. B. (2025b). *Governing Babel: The Debate over Social Media Platforms and Free Speech – and What Comes Next*. Cambridge, MA: MIT Press.

Yeung, K. and Bygrave, L. A. (2021). Demystifying the Modernized European Data Protection Regime: Cross-Disciplinary Insights from Legal and Regulatory Governance Scholarship. *Regulation & Governance*, 16: 137–155.

Zeng, J. and Kaye, D. B. V. (2022). From Content Moderation to Visibility Moderation: A Case Study of Platform Governance on TikTok. *Policy & Internet*, 14(1): 79–95. https://doi.org/10.1002/poi3.287.

Acknowledgements

We would like to thank Megan Richardson for her careful shepherding of this Element towards publication. Her editing and advice (including especially on legal aspects) helped bring our arguments to life. She is a valued mentor and colleague who has played a key role in our academic lives, and we cannot thank her enough.

We are also grateful to Andrea Carson, Damian Clifford, Peter Coe, Simon Chesterman, Silvia Montaña-Niño, Frank Pasquale and Jeannie Paterson, who generously read drafts of this Element. They offered valuable comments, shared their perspectives and challenged our beliefs, which helped us refine this Element for the better. Thi Thu Ha Do also provided most helpful research support. We are especially grateful to our two anonymous reviewers for their invaluable insights and feedback on drafts of this Element.

James further recognises the wider scholarly community in Australia. Conversations across multiple seminars, coffees and conferences have been vital in shaping his views. He has occasionally used ChatGPT to check points and refine language. Corinne is grateful to the legal research community in Australia and in Singapore, and appreciates the views she has garnered from workshops, chats and conversations, which has helped fuel her interest in writing on contemporary topics such as this. She is thankful for the support received both from the Division of Business Law at Nanyang Technological University and the Centre for Technology, Robotics, Artificial Intelligence and the Law at the National University of Singapore. Of course, all factual and legal propositions, arguments, interpretations and intellectual contributions in this Element are the authors' own responsibility.

Finally, we would like to thank the ARC Centre of Excellence for Automated Decision Making and Society, and its Director Julian Thomas, for making this collaboration possible.

This work was supported by the Australian Research Council Grant CE200100005 and FT230100475.

Cambridge Elements

Data Rights and Wrongs

Damian Clifford
Australian National University

Damian Clifford is an Assistant Professor at the London School of Economics and Political Science. Previously a Senior Lecturer and Postdoctoral Research Fellow at the Australian National University, and FWO Aspirant Fellow at KU Leuven's Centre for IT and IP Law (CiTiP), his research focuses on data protection, privacy and technology regulation, and he has published across these fields. His recent books are *Data Rights and Private Law* (ed with Jeannie Marie Paterson and Kwan Ho Lau, 2023); *Data Protection Law and Emotions* (2024); and *Data Rights in Transition* (with Rachelle Bosua, Jing Qian and Megan Richardson, 2025).

Jeannie Marie Paterson
University of Melbourne

Jeannie Marie Paterson is Director of the Centre for AI and Digital Ethics at the University of Melbourne and a Professor of Law at the Melbourne Law School. Her research focuses on themes of support for vulnerable consumers; the regulation of new technologies in consumer and financial markets; and regulatory design for protecting consumer rights and promoting safe, fair and accountable technologies. Her recent books include *Misleading Silence* (ed with Elise Bant, 2020); and *Data Rights and Private Law* (ed with Damian Clifford and Kwan Ho Lau, 2023).

Editorial Board

About the Series

This Cambridge Elements series provides a home for fresh arguments about data rights and wrongs along with legal, ethical and other responses. We encourage new ways of thinking about data as enmeshed within social, institutional and technical relations.

Cambridge Elements

Data Rights and Wrongs

Elements in the Series

Data Rights in Transition
Rachelle Bosua, Damian Clifford, Jing Qian and Megan Richardson

Data Access and AI Explainability
Frank Pasquale

Addressing Misinformation and Disinformation
James Meese and Corinne Tan

A full series listing is available at: www.cambridge.org/EDRW

Printed by Integrated Books International,
United States of America